DIM SUM

FUN GOR with cilantro

DIM SUM

THE ART OF CHINESE TEA LUNCH

written and illustrated by

ELLEN LEONG BLONDER

CLARKSON POTTER/PUBLISHERS

New York

ALSO BY ELLEN LEONG BLONDER

Every Grain of Rice:
A Taste of Our Chinese Childhood in America (with Annabel Low)

Published by Clarkson Potter/Publishers,
New York, New York.
Member of the Crown Publishing Group.

Random House, Inc. New York, Toronto, London,
Sydney, Auckland

CLARKSON N. POTTER is a trademark and
POTTER and colophon are registered trademarks
of Random House, Inc.

Printed in China

Design by Marysarah Quinn

Library of Congress Cataloging-in-Publication Data
Blonder, Ellen, 1950–
Dim sum: the art of Chinese tea lunch / by
Ellen Blonder—1st ed.
Includes bibliographical references and index.
1. Cookery, Chinese.   2. Dim sum.
3. Dumplings. I. Title.
TX724.5.C5 B5697   2002
641.5951—dc21   2001035956

ISBN 0-609-60887-8

10 9 8 7 6 5 4 3 2 1

FIRST EDITION

TO NICK,

who continues to touch my heart,

and

TO MY PARENTS,

for everything

ACKNOWLEDGMENTS

My love and thanks to my parents, whose gentle assistance and advice and hours of tireless testing, translating, and tasting reminded me of gifts they gave all their children: curiosity, determination, and appreciation for good food.

Thanks to my husband, Nick, who not only accompanied me on almost all my restaurant forays and was my guinea pig for every home-cooked experiment, but who also listened to and encouraged me throughout. And thanks to our daughter, Lisa, who was my number one vegetarian taster and adviser.

Thanks to other family, who tasted and shared memories and recipes: Dewey, Carolyn (and her mother), Edmond, Julie, Bob, David, Toni, Dennis, Esther, Wynne, and all their children. Special thanks to Annabel, who used all she learned from writing *Every Grain of Rice* together to help, encourage, and laugh with me.

Thanks to my agent, Amy Rennert, for taking my idea and running with it with faith and enthusiasm; to my editor, Pam Krauss, for seeing the possibilities immediately and for exercising tremendous skill and care; and to art director Marysarah Quinn, for her design acumen, sensitivity, and open mind.

Many thanks to friends—from sea-soned dim sum fans to the uninitiated—who tasted and offered opinions on restaurant and home-cooked dishes: Rita Abrams, Mia Antonelli, Elspeth Martin, Carol Ring, Marthine Satris, Justin Scheuenstuhl, Patricia and Jennifer Schwarz, Wendy Slick, Emmy, Sam, and Martin Cruz Smith, and Sarah Watkins.

And thanks to friends, acquaintances, and restaurant employees who took the time to offer travel and restaurant tips and helpful advice: Tane Chan, Tony Chan, Michele Anna Jordan, Chi Fat Luk, Elaine Woo Neiman, Jenny Petrone, Michael Sanson, Sharon Silva, Martin Yan, and Allan Yung.

BAMBOO STEAMER

CONTENTS

FLAT-LEAVED CHINESE CHIVES

TOUCHING THE HEART

BROCCOLI

Dim sum translates loosely as "touch the heart," which is just what the myriad morsels of a dim sum meal do. While dim sum is usually thought of as a Cantonese specialty, dishes come from many regions: pancakes from the northwest and buns from the north, for example. What began as a mid- to late-afternoon snack has become more often a breakfast or lunch; few restaurants serve dim sum for dinner, although some now offer it well into the wee hours.

At a busy dim sum restaurant, waitresses jam the aisles with carts bearing small samplings of delicacies, calling out their offerings in operatic singsong. Some carts are piled high with individual steamer baskets; others are fitted with bins to keep stews or rice porridges hot. Still others have griddle tops for pan-frying dishes to order, or glass cases displaying shelves of glistening pastries. On some carts, plastic signs announce the contents, so diners, too eager to wait until a waitress is within earshot, can flag her down.

Yum cha means "drink tea," or, more accurately, to have a tea breakfast or lunch with dim sum food. When I was very young, I used to think having tea and dim sum was the activity of idle, bejeweled ladies pausing in a day of mah-jongg, or of older men sharing a long breakfast over a Chinese newspaper and the latest gossip. After all, the only effort one needed to expend was to beckon a waitress and then nod or wave her away. One could eat for hours from a never-ending parade of carts, the waitresses placing dish after dish on the table.

When I started searching for a dim sum book that included my favorite dishes, I was surprised to find how few existed. Some books contained impossibly elaborate recipes or off-putting ingredients—snow toad fat or plaster of Paris, for instance. Others provided vague or scant English translations. I became intrigued by the idea of writing and illustrating my own. I had grown up making a few kinds of dim sum alongside older relatives, but there were many dishes I had been eating for years, and I wanted to know how they were made.

I grew up within a large constellation of immigrant relatives, and everyone cooked. On a farm far away from Chinatown, we had to make our own dumplings if we wanted dim sum. After helping to make sixty or seventy shrimp dumplings, we children might be rewarded with leftover wheat starch dough to fashion into lumpy swans to float on soy sauce puddles. At that young age, our fingers learned when dough had the right texture, while our palates became familiar with the complex flavors of dim sum. Those early lessons served as the foundation for this book.

I consulted dozens of cookbooks, recruiting my parents to translate those written in Chinese. Their curiosity was piqued. Cooking test results flew back and forth, and my seventy-nine-year-old father sent me a thirty-page list of food words and cooking terms he wrote on his computer—in English, *pinyin* Mandarin, Cantonese, and in Chinese characters. My mother queried older relatives and neighbors for techniques and advice. I coaxed friends and family into dozens of dim sum restaurants in my local San Francisco area, Los Angeles, Vancouver, and Hong Kong.

One restaurateur proudly told me that on a weekend his restaurant offered more than 100 different dim sum dishes, and that seven men were employed just to make dumplings. Lest this make the prospect of homemade dim sum seem like an overwhelming challenge, bear in mind that no one eats 100 varieties in one sitting.

Most dumpling recipes in this book make about two dozen. If that seems like too many, you may be surprised at how quickly they disappear. Should you have leftovers, keep in mind that many dumplings freeze beautifully. Most need only a final quick cooking, so it is possible to serve a variety of dumplings without working yourself into a frazzle. A few premade dumplings also make a delightful treat in the middle of a busy workweek or an easy last-minute appetizer.

DISHES TO MAKE AHEAD

These can be made ahead and frozen:
+ All steamed dumplings (pages 24–36); except Seafood Soup Dumplings
+ Boiled Beef Dumplings (page 42)
+ Fish Dumplings (page 44)
+ All potstickers (pages 48–51)
+ All bao (steamed, pages 53–55 and 124–25, or baked, pages 58–59 and 123; except Pan-Fried Bao)
+ Char Siu Pastries (page 66)
+ Savory Turnovers (page 68)
+ Rice in Lotus Leaf Packets (page 73)

These can be partially prepared a day ahead or early in the day:
+ All greens (pages 85–89)
+ Turnip Cake (page 90)
+ Char Siu (page 114)
+ Steamed Spareribs (page 115)
+ Beef Meatballs (page 116)
+ Beef Stew (page 118)
+ Almond Pudding (page 121)
+ Mango Pudding (page 122)
+ All sauces and condiments (pages 133–37)

Every recipe has been tested, a few for days on end, and some never made it into the book—or even as far as the dining table. Some dim sum aficionados are bound to notice the absence of chicken feet and other personal favorites, but with limited space and time, I chose dishes that I hoped would appeal to a wide audience, using mostly ingredients that were readily available.

Tea lunch is a tradition that goes back many centuries, but it has continued to evolve throughout that time. In that spirit, I decided to include vegetarian alternatives or lower-fat substitutions to appeal to current health-conscious attitudes.

Many dishes can be made ahead and frozen, including all the steamed dumplings (except the Seafood Soup Dumplings), boiled dumplings, potstickers, steamed or baked bao, and savory pastries. In addition, many dishes can be prepared a day ahead or early in the day, as noted throughout the book. (See the complete list on page 9.)

For those who are familiar with the ingredients, techniques, and flavors of dim sum, I hope you will be encouraged to try new dishes as well as your favorites. For novices, many of these recipes can be made entirely from ingredients available at most well-stocked supermarkets. A resource section includes places to order both groceries and equipment.

Yum cha!

A FEW WORDS ABOUT RESTAURANTS

A first visit to a dim sum restaurant, especially a big one, can be a daunting experience, so a few pointers are in order.

Dim sum brunch or lunch is often a family affair, so weekends, especially Sundays, are the busiest days. You can gauge the expected wait for a table by the overflow crowds outside, the number of chairs packed into the waiting area, and the presence of a microphone to call out reservation numbers. Arriving before eleven will improve your chances of getting a table without a long wait. Go to the receptionist immediately to put your name on the waiting list; you will be given a number. Many large restaurants can seat 800 to 1,000 people, so the wait may not be as long as it looks. Don't worry if you hear numbers being called in Chinese; if you request a table in English, your number will be called in English, too. Also, numbers are not necessarily called in sequence, since the size of your party affects the availability of a table.

Once you are seated, you will be asked to choose a tea, and a pot will be brought to your table immediately. Sometimes a restaurant will offer an English language menu, which may even contain photographs to help you order. At the other extreme are Chinese-only menus, on which you put check marks next to the dishes you want.

More often, instead of a menu, a card with a blank grid will be placed at your table to be marked by servers throughout your meal. Waitresses will stroll the aisles pushing carts or bearing trays and calling out the names of their dishes. Wave a waitress over when you think you want something. Don't be shy about asking her to open a steamer for a peek or an explanation before you say yes—or no.

Once you have indicated you would like a dish, the waitress will put it on your table and mark your card in the appropriate spot. The card will have sections for small, medium, and large dishes, their prices based on the elaborateness of preparation or expense of the ingredients. All dishes in a category will be the same price. Other sections cover beverages and special-order dishes.

Another possibility, although it doesn't happen much anymore, is that instead of using a card, your waiter will simply count the number of plates on your table at the end of your meal and multiply that by the price per plate. Different-sized or -colored plates tell the waiter whether to count the dish at the small, medium, or large price.

Occasionally a restaurant will have a waitress at a side table pan-frying dim sum dishes on the spot for you to take back to your table; take your card with you to have it marked when you receive your order. At a large, busy restaurant it is not unheard

Tip the teapot lid askew to signal for more tea.

Your card is marked as you order.

of for overeager diners to swarm around a waitress as she pushes a full cart out the kitchen door, grabbing dishes off her cart and waving their cards in her face to have them marked.

If you've never had a dim sum meal before, pace yourself. Invariably, some intriguing dish will roll out of the kitchen after you've had your fill, or seen the same dumplings make their rounds over and over. Don't forget, on a busy weekend, a large restaurant may offer more than 100 varieties. If you know what you want, you can usually special-order something on the menu or have a waiter track it down in the kitchen.

Don't wait to amass your whole meal before you dig in. Part of the fun of dim sum is having something hot almost as soon as you sit down, and adding from an endless variety as the meal progresses. I've been westernized enough to save sweet dishes for last, but you needn't.

Condiments may or may not be on the table. Taste a dumpling before you drown it in soy sauce, because a well-seasoned dumpling should not need more salt. Sometimes hot mustard, chili oil, or a dipping sauce containing ginger, vinegar, or scallions may be served to enhance a specific dish.

A dim sum meal is fun to share with friends; the more diners, the more varieties you can sample. An order usually contains two to six pieces, so you may want to take multiple orders to ensure that everyone gets a taste. An etiquette trick is to flip your chopsticks upside down and use the top end to place something on a fellow diner's plate or break a dumpling in half to share. Turn the chopsticks back over to eat, so that only one end goes into your mouth.

You will almost surely finish your first pot of tea as you eat. When your teapot needs refilling, simply tip the lid askew. A sharp-eyed waiter will either come by with a kettleful of boiling water or take your teapot away and bring it back refilled. A double tap of your index and middle finger on the table or the side of your teacup subtly signals a thank-you for the refill.

You may order a little or a lot. Dim sum makes excellent fast food; it's also a wonderful way to have a long, leisurely meal. I've ordered as few as three dishes for a quick, light lunch and been in and out of a restaurant in less than a half hour. Other times I've arrived early, stayed until the lunch crowd thinned, and selected so many dishes that even a waitress couldn't resist telling me she thought I had ordered enough.

Finally, remember that no one can sample all of a restaurant's delicacies in one sitting, so look forward to returning another day with a fresh palate.

THE ROLE OF TEA

Legend has tea being discovered accidentally around 3000 B.C., when tea leaves blew into an outdoor cooking vessel being used to boil water. It was immediately appreciated for its refreshing flavor, and the eventual discovery of its medicinal value and ability to enhance alertness led to its increased use.

Tea was brewed from fresh leaves until the third century B.C., when drying and processing tremendously widened its popularity. Tea has been cultivated commercially in China for at least 1,800 years. Through the centuries, it has served as currency, as payment of taxes to emperors, and as a key factor in the development of porcelain, world trade, and international relations.

While the earliest teahouses served nothing but tea, that gradually changed. Starting with nuts and seeds, accompaniments became more and more elaborate, until "having tea" came to connote enjoying a meal at which dim sum played the central role.

Tea has evolved, too, into countless varieties, but every tea can still be classified as belonging to one of three categories: green, semi-fermented, or black (called red in China). All come from the same shrub, *Camellia sinensis*. Differences arise from processing techniques. Leaves for green tea are either wilted or not, then pan-fried, steamed, or fired in an oven to prevent oxidation and enzyme action. Leaves for semi-fermented and black teas are wilted, then bruised to allow oxidation to different degrees; this triggers enzymes to create chemical changes, producing tea with more color and less astringency. A final firing stops the process and dries the leaves.

Further variations in tea result from differing soils, climates, time of year the leaves are picked, which leaves are picked, whether leaves are wilted in the sun or shade, and whether flowers or other ingredients are added to scent the tea.

CHOOSING A TEA

The first question you will be asked when you are seated at a dim sum restaurant is, "What tea will you have?" Here are some favorites you may want to try, either at a restaurant or at home:

DRAGON WELL, OR LUNG CHING, is a mellow green tea celebrated for its bright color and cooling effect. The highest grade is picked from tiny, very young buds and leaves, then dried flat, and the skill required to process them contributes to its high cost.

GUNPOWDER, OR PINGSHUI, is a strong green tea named for the pelletlike shape of its tightly rolled leaves. It is also known as pearl tea, or *zhucha*, because of its appearance.

JASMINE, OR MOLI HUACHA, is a green or semi-fermented oolong tea with jasmine flowers added. It is refreshingly astringent, with a delicate flower fragrance; the oolong variety is fuller, with a more lingering after-taste. Jasmine is often the default tea you will be given if you don't make a choice.

KEEMUN, OR QIHONG, is known as the king or champagne of black teas, for its roselike fra-grance, slightly smoky taste, and deep amber color.

LYCHEE, OR LIZHI HONGCHA, is a black tea scented with the juice of lychee fruit, which also gives it a sweet, mellow, flowery aroma.

OOLONG refers to a group of semi-fermented teas, less astringent than green teas, with a floral aftertaste. These include *ti kwan yin* and some jasmine teas.

PU-ERH (also pronounced *po nay* or *bo lay*), a semi-fermented tea, is a popular dim sum tea because of its reputed ability to counter-act rich food and reduce cholesterol. This is the tea I order if I plan to indulge in deep-fried dim sum. It has an earthy, mellow flavor.

TI KWAN YIN (also spelled *tieguanyin*), the Iron Goddess of Mercy, lends her name to this most famous oolong tea, prized for its orchidlike aroma.

TI KWAN YIN TEA LEAVES

BREWING TEA

There are many disagreements about how to brew perfect tea, with different opinions on correct water temperature, whether to use a tea ball or tea bags, how long to steep or infuse the tea, how much tea to use, and whether to reuse the leaves for a second pot. You will no doubt develop your own preferences, but for starters, here are some suggestions.

For the freshest-tasting tea, start with cold water in your kettle. While it is boiling, fill your teapot with hot water to warm it. Just before the water boils, empty the teapot and measure about 1 teaspoon of tea leaves into the pot for each cup of water you plan to use. If you use a perforated metal tea ball, do not overfill it, because the leaves need room to expand.

Pour the boiling water directly over the leaves and steep them for 3 to 5 minutes. (Some people first "wash" the dry tea leaves with a little boiling water, pouring it off immediately, then filling the pot with fresh boiling water.) Green teas require less steeping time than semi-fermented and black teas. Stronger tea is made by using more leaves, not more time. Longer steeping may result in bitter tea, so you may want to transfer the tea to another heated pot or, as many Chinese households do, to a heated thermos.

I don't mind a few tea leaves in the bottom of my cup, but if you're fussier, use a tea strainer when you pour your tea into the cup.

More boiling water may be added to the teapot for a second infusion. In fact, some connoisseurs insist the second infusion is best.

With a Chinese meal, whether to serve tea with or after the food is a regional preference, but tea is *always* served with dim sum. In any case, never add sugar, milk, or lemon to the tea.

STEAMED DUMPLINGS

PORK CHINESE CHIVE DUMPLINGS

When most people think of dim sum, they probably think of dumplings first. Coax a waitress to lift the lids from the stacked steamers on her cart and you'll be tantalized by translucent wheat starch dumplings with myriad fillings—delectable mouthfuls of pork, shrimp, scallops, or vegetables. Most dumplings are steamed, their wrappers cleverly twisted and pleated into fanciful shapes. The most common, *ha gow*, is instantly recognizable by its delicately pleated exterior. *Siu mai* shows off its filling above a ruffled collar. Other dumplings are folded into triangles, crescents, and twisted circles.

SETTING UP A STEAMER

Most steamed dishes are cooked over rapidly boiling water; the plate of food is kept elevated on a stand above the water level. The pot must be large enough to allow steam to circulate around the plate, and the pot should have a tight-fitting lid. A wok with a high, domed lid or a wide pasta pot can work well as a steamer.

If you plan to steam a lot, invest in a multitiered metal or bamboo steamer from Chinatown. Aluminum or stainless steel steamers have a bottom section to hold water, two tiers with perforated bottoms for steam to circulate through, and a tight lid. Advantages of a metal steamer are that the bottom section can double as a pot, and it is the best choice for steaming buns.

Bamboo steamer baskets are meant to fit snugly over an open wok filled with boiling water. The bottom of each tier is made from bamboo slats; the sides are fashioned from several layers of split bamboo lashed together. The ingeniously woven top holds in steam remarkably well; it is used instead of a wok lid. Advantages of bamboo steamers are that they impart a wonderful, subtle scent; they work as well as metal steamers for steaming buns; and they are pretty enough to hang on the wall or double as baskets. They also seem to improve with age; mine have lasted many years.

POT AND STAND

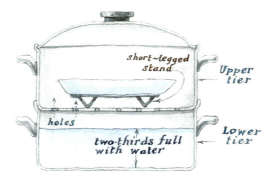

TIERED METAL STEAMER

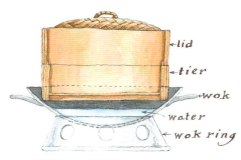

BAMBOO STEAMER AND WOK

HELPFUL STEAMING GADGETS

Metal stands of varying dimensions are available in Chinatown. Most have three legs holding up a metal ring on which a plate rests. A large plate can be held aloft by a short-legged stand to keep it from blocking the perforated bottom of a steamer tier. Some inserts are designed just for woks. One looks like a bamboo tic-tac-toe grid. Another is a perforated metal disk that fits halfway into the wok, with room above for a plate and the wok lid, and room below for an ample quantity of water.

You can create makeshift stands, too. A plate may balance on a pair of chopsticks laid inside your wok. A tuna or bamboo shoot can with both ends cut out is the right height to support a plate inside a wok or pot.

A plate lifter from Chinatown is one of my favorite inexpensive gadgets for a steamer, and it's equipment I consider essential. Three prongs spread out to hook around the edge of most plates, allowing you to lift it straight up out of a hot steamer instead of having to slide an unwieldy oven mitt down alongside the plate, perhaps causing its contents to spill. Be sure to support your plate from underneath with a mitt or potholder once it clears the steamer.

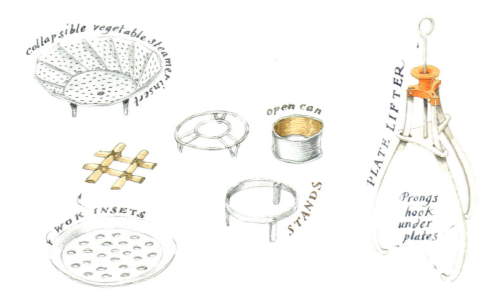

collapsible vegetable steamer insert

open can

WOK INSETS

STANDS

PLATE LIFTER

Prongs
hook
under
plates

To steam foods, add water to the pot or wok to a depth of about 1½ to 2 inches. If you are using a steamer, fill the bottom section two-thirds full with water.

Bring the water to a boil. Place the pan or plate of food on the stand in a pot or wok and cover it with a lid. If using a steamer, place the plate of food on a tier and stack the steamer together. Steam the food over high heat. Replenish the pot with boiling water as necessary between batches, and check the water level from time to time for dishes that require long cooking times.

WHAT'S IN A DOUGH?

Most of the dumplings in this book use one of two basic dumpling doughs, and they're quite different even though they're both derived from wheat. The flour dough is just all-purpose flour and water—essentially a pasta dough. The gluten in the flour gives it resilience, so it can be rolled very thin or stretched without tearing, and it is easily pinched closed. It is sturdy enough to withstand pan-frying, deep-frying, and boiling. The dough remains opaque, and you may vary its color and flavor by adding egg yolk, curry powder, or puréed spinach or carrots.

The other basic dumpling dough is made with wheat starch and a bit of tapi-oca flour. This dough is more fragile and tender than flour dough, and it is prone to splitting open during steaming if it is not carefully pinched closed. Still, this is the dough that becomes a translucent jewel case when steamed, and its lightness will not overwhelm a delicate filling.

The wrappers carried by many supermarkets are made from flour dough, and though they may be labeled with different names, the primary difference is how thinly they are rolled. A one-pound package will contain about 20 spring roll wrappers, 40 to 60 potsticker wrappers, or at least 80 thinner siu mai wrappers. Square wonton wrappers are too thin to use in place of potsticker wrappers, but they work as siu mai wrappers; you may trim them into circles with a cookie cutter or use them as is.

A fanciful array of dumpling shapes and colors contributes as much to their appeal as the variety of fillings within. Traditionally, certain fillings go with certain folds; ha gow, for instance, are immediately recognizable by their shape. Still, I've had "ha gow" filled with pea shoots, so feel free to experiment with different combinations.

Once you have shaped and filled the dumplings, take care to pinch the edges together very tightly to seal in the filling and keep the dough from breaking open during cooking.

MAKING WHEAT STARCH DUMPLINGS AHEAD AND FREEZING

Wheat starch dumplings should be cooked, then cooled before freezing. Flour dumplings should be frozen *before* cooking, whether they are to be steamed, boiled, or pan-fried. Most dumplings will keep for at least 2 to 3 weeks in the freezer if very well wrapped.

Arrange cooked, cooled wheat starch dumplings slightly apart on a parchment-lined baking sheet. Cover the baking sheet loosely with foil and freeze until the dumplings are firm, about 2 hours. Transfer them to a plastic bag, squeeze out as much air as possible, and seal. To reheat, arrange frozen dumplings ½ inch apart in oiled pans, thaw at room temperature, and then steam them for 4 to 5 minutes to heat through.

Arrange shaped, filled, uncooked flour dumplings slightly apart on a floured, parchment-lined baking sheet. Cover loosely with foil and freeze until the dumplings are firm, about 2 hours. Transfer to a plastic bag, squeeze out as much air as possible, and seal.

To serve, boil flour dumplings without thawing, adding 2 to 3 minutes to the cooking time. Test for doneness by removing a dumpling and cutting it in half to make sure the filling is hot and cooked through.

To steam flour dumplings, arrange frozen dumplings ½ inch apart in oiled pans, thaw at room temperature, and then steam as directed in the recipe.

Set potstickers slightly apart on a floured baking sheet and thaw at room temperature for 30 minutes. Pan-fry for 3 to 4 minutes; then add ½ cup plus 1 tablespoon water, cover, and cook as directed in the recipe, increasing the cooking time to 7 to 8 minutes. Uncover and continue cooking 2 to 3 minutes, until all the liquid has evaporated and the bottoms of the dumplings are crisp.

WHEAT STARCH DOUGH

When you want translucent steamed dumplings, this is the dough to use. Make fillings ahead so they can cool while you make the dough. Knead the dough as soon as you can handle it; the boiling water must reach every bit of starch. The dough cannot be made ahead and refrigerated, as it becomes more prone to splitting open during steaming. The dough will appear somewhat mottled and opaque when it is first removed from the steamer, but it becomes magically translucent as it cools.

MAKES TWENTY-FOUR 3¼-INCH WRAPPERS

1¼ cups wheat starch plus ¼ cup tapioca
  flour, or 1½ cups wheat starch (see
  Note)
½ teaspoon salt
1 cup boiling water
1 teaspoon peanut or vegetable oil

In a medium bowl, combine the wheat starch, tapioca flour, if using, and salt. Add the boiling water and the oil and stir with chopsticks or a wooden spoon. While the dough is still very hot, turn it out onto a board dusted with 1 tablespoon of wheat starch. Knead until smooth, adding a little more wheat starch if necessary. The dough should be soft but not sticky.

Divide the dough into thirds. Use your palms to roll each portion into an 8-inch cylinder. Cover loosely with a slightly damp paper towel to keep the dough from drying out. The dough is now ready to cut and press or roll out as needed.

NOTE: You may use all wheat starch, but the addition of tapioca flour seems to help sealed edges stick together better. Tapioca flour is sometimes labeled tapioca starch.

To make round dumpling wrappers, wheat starch dough can be sandwiched between squares of baking parchment and then pressed flat using downward pressure on the flat side of a cleaver blade or the flat bottom of a pan. The result will be an almost-perfect circle. Afterward, if you still want your circles larger or a little thinner, roll them out lightly with a rolling pin before peeling away the parchment.

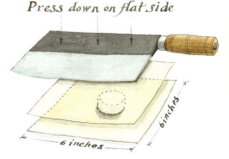

Press down on flat side

6 inches
6 inches

3¼ inches

FLOUR DOUGH

These all-purpose flour-based wrappers are a dim sum staple. Although packaged potsticker wrappers and siu mai wrappers are easy to come by, homemade wrappers will be more elastic, with a bit more body, and the edges will not require moistening before sealing. Spinach, carrot, or curry add flavor and color for even greater versatility. The same dough, made with a bit less water and cut into large squares can be used for spring rolls.

Roll, shape, and fill one dumpling at a time until you are adept enough to work very quickly, because the rolled-out dough becomes overly elastic when it rests too long.

MAKES TWENTY-FOUR 3¼-INCH WRAPPERS

¾ cup all-purpose flour, plus additional for dusting the board

In a medium bowl, mix ¾ cup flour with ⅓ cup water until combined. Turn out onto a generously floured board and knead for 3 to 4 minutes, or until smooth. The dough should be fairly stiff. Form the dough into a 9-inch cylinder; then cut it in half crosswise. Dust the dough with flour, cover it loosely with plastic wrap, and let it rest at room temperature for 20 minutes.

On a lightly floured board, use your palms to roll each cylinder out to about 12 inches. The dough is now ready to cut and roll as needed. Keep the unused portion loosely covered with plastic wrap or an overturned bowl as you work to prevent it from drying out.

Unlike wheat starch dough, flour dough needs to be rolled out with a rolling pin. I think a slight variation in the circles is part of the charm of handmade dumplings, but for more uniform dumplings, you may use a cookie cutter to cut 3- to 3¼-inch circles out of rolled-out dough. A tuna or bamboo shoot can with both ends cut out makes a good 3¼-inch cutter.

VARIATIONS
EGG DOUGH

To make a slightly yellower dough, lightly beat 1 large egg yolk with enough water to make ⅓ cup. Mix with the flour and proceed as above.

SPINACH DOUGH

This green dough works for steamed, boiled, and pan-fried dumplings, and its color contrasts beautifully with a variety of fillings, especially bright orange shrimp in siu mai.

Place 1 cup (2 ounces raw) packed spinach leaves (no stems) with 1 tablespoon water over low heat until just wilted. Without squeezing the spinach out, place it in a measuring cup with enough water to make ⅓ cup. Transfer to a blender and blend to a thick purée. Transfer the purée to a bowl, mix in the flour, and then turn the dough out onto a lightly floured board and knead it until the spinach is distributed throughout the dough. Proceed as on page 22.

CARROT DOUGH

Carrot dough is best for steamed or pan-fried dumplings; boiling, however, diffuses both its flavor and color.

Boil a peeled and chunked medium carrot for 8 minutes, or until soft. Weigh out 1 ounce carrot and add water to make ⅓ cup. Purée in a blender until smooth. Transfer to a bowl, mix in the flour, and then turn the dough out onto a lightly floured board and knead it until the carrot is well blended in the dough. Proceed as on page 22.

CURRY DOUGH

While curry dough is good for boiled and steamed dumplings, it's superb for potstickers because pan-frying enhances both the flavor and aroma of the curry. Stir 1¼ teaspoons curry powder into the flour before adding the water. Proceed as on page 22.

SPRING ROLL WRAPPERS

MAKES 8 WRAPPERS

1½ cups all-purpose flour, plus additional for dusting the board
½ teaspoon salt
2 large egg yolks

Sift the flour and salt together into a medium bowl. Put the egg yolks in a measuring cup and add enough water to make ½ cup. Beat the mixture lightly; then stir it into the flour to make a stiff dough, adding a few drops of water at a time, if necessary. Turn the dough out onto a floured surface and knead it for 3 to 4 minutes, or until smooth. Using your palms, roll the dough into an 8-inch cylinder. Dust the dough with flour, cover it loosely with plastic wrap, and let it rest for 20 minutes.

Cut the dough crosswise into eight 1-inch pieces. Keep the unused portion loosely covered with plastic wrap or an overturned bowl to keep it from drying out. On a floured board, roll out each piece to about 6½ inches square. Trim off the uneven edges to make a 6-inch square. Cover the wrapper loosely with plastic wrap. Repeat with the remaining dough. Proceed as directed for Spring Rolls (page 105).

HA GOW

An order of these popular dumplings reveals much about a restaurant: whether the kitchen uses a generous proportion of succulent shrimp or an overabundance of cheaper bamboo shoots, whether the wrappers are artfully pleated or so soggy the filling falls out. Good ha gow often indicate the other dim sum will be good also, so I always order them in an unfamiliar restaurant.

Although most of the dumpling recipes that follow make about 24 dumplings, ha gow are traditionally smaller, so one recipe of wheat starch dough and filling will yield 32. A pointed grapefruit spoon makes a good tool for spooning filling into the small opening.

MAKES 32 DUMPLINGS

FILLING

8 ounces medium shrimp, peeled and
    deveined, cut into ½-inch chunks
3 tablespoons minced bamboo shoots
½ teaspoon soy sauce
¼ teaspoon salt
1 teaspoon rice wine or dry sherry
⅛ teaspoon ground white pepper
½ teaspoon toasted sesame oil
1 tablespoon cornstarch

Wheat Starch Dough (page 21), rolled into
    four 8-inch cylinders

Mix the filling ingredients and set aside. Oil several 8- or 9-inch round cake pans.

Cut each cylinder of wheat starch dough crosswise into 8 pieces. Put one piece of dough, cut side up, between two 6-inch squares of baking parchment; then position the flat side of a cleaver blade or a flat bottom of a pan over it and press straight down to form a 3-inch circle. Peel off the parchment.

Make one very narrow pleat that extends from the edge almost all the way to the center of the circle. Make 7 or 8 more narrow pleats alongside, each almost overlapping the last. Your final pleat should be just over halfway around the circumference of the dough. Press a finger lightly along the inside of the pleats to flatten them slightly and enlarge the pocket within. Spoon about a teaspoon of the filling into the pocket, keeping it from touching the open edge of the dough. Pinch the edges of the dough together very firmly. Repeat with the remaining dough and filling. Arrange the finished dumplings ½ inch apart in the oiled pans.

Set up a steamer and bring the water to a boil. Steam the dumplings over high heat for 7 minutes, replenishing the pot with boiling water as necessary between batches. Let the dumplings rest for a few minutes before transferring them to a serving plate. Serve hot.

SCALLOP DUMPLINGS

Because of their cost, scallops were not every-day fare in my home, but on the banquet table, I've always looked for them eagerly, their delicate sweetness usually combined with mild vegetables. In these dumplings, a few scallops, mixed with finely diced vegetables spiked with a little ginger and garlic, go a long way.

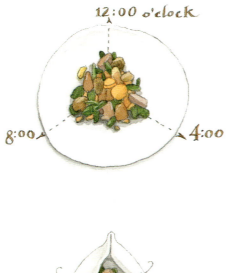

MAKES 24 DUMPLINGS

2 teaspoons peanut or vegetable oil
¼ cup finely diced carrot
¼ cup finely diced celery
¼ cup finely diced water chestnuts
2 to 3 garlic cloves, minced
2 teaspoons finely diced peeled fresh
    ginger
10 ounces scallops, cut in ¼-inch dice
1 teaspoon soy sauce
1 teaspoon salt
1 teaspoon rice wine
⅛ teaspoon ground white pepper
1 teaspoon toasted sesame oil
1 teaspoon cornstarch

Wheat Starch Dough (page 21)

Heat a wok or skillet; then add the peanut oil. When it is almost smoking, add the carrot, celery, water chestnuts, garlic, and ginger and stir-fry for 2 minutes over medium heat. Transfer the mixture to a bowl and let it cool; then stir in the

remaining ingredients until thoroughly combined. Cover and refrigerate.

Oil several 8- or 9-inch round cake pans.

Cut each cylinder of wheat starch dough crosswise into 8 pieces. Put one piece of dough, cut side up, between two 6-inch squares of baking parchment; then position the flat side of a cleaver blade or a flat bottom of a pan over it and press straight down to form a 3¼-inch circle. Peel off the parchment.

Spoon about 2 teaspoons of the filling onto the center of the circle of dough, leaving enough margin to pinch the edges together. Pinch the edges together starting from

3 equidistant points (imagine a clock at 12, 4, and 8 o'clock) around the circle until the edges meet in the middle. Pinch the center point firmly, taking care not to tear the dough. Repeat with the remaining dough and filling. Arrange the finished dumplings ½ inch apart in the oiled pans.

Set up a steamer and bring the water to a boil. Steam the dumplings for 8 minutes over high heat, replenishing the pot with boiling water as necessary between batches. Let the dumplings rest for a few minutes before transferring them to a serving plate. Serve hot.

SCALLOP DUMPLINGS

CRAB DUMPLINGS

This dumpling borrows its gathered crescent fold from traditional shark's fin dumplings. Shark's fin is so costly and time consuming to process, however, that restaurants often use only a few token shreds—barely enough to taste. Instead, I prefer this crabmeat filling paired with shrimp to give it body. Although this may be made with packaged wrappers, it's prettier and more substantial if you take the time to make the spinach dough.

MAKES ABOUT 24 DUMPLINGS

FILLING

4 ounces lump crabmeat, picked over for
    cartilage and shredded
8 ounces shrimp, peeled, deveined, and
    coarsely ground or chopped
1 scallion (white and green parts), finely
    sliced
2 teaspoons finely minced fresh cilantro
    (optional)
1 large egg, lightly beaten
1 teaspoon soy sauce
½ teaspoon salt
1 teaspoon rice wine or dry sherry
¼ teaspoon sugar
1 teaspoon toasted sesame oil
2 teaspoons cornstarch

Spinach Dough (page 22) or 24 to 28
    packaged siu mai wrappers

Mix the filling ingredients together and refrigerate the mixture for at least 30 minutes or up to 2 hours before using.

Oil several 8- or 9-inch round cake pans.

If using homemade wrappers, cut each cylinder of dough into 12 pieces. On a floured board, use a rolling pin to roll one piece to a 3¼-inch circle.

Spoon a heaping teaspoon of the filling onto the center of the circle of dough, leaving enough margin to pinch closed. If using packaged wrappers, dip a finger in water and run it all around the top edge. Fold the dumpling into a semicircle and pinch the edges together tightly.

On a flat surface, place the crescent with its pinched edges up. Gather the dough into irregular folds all along the top edge and pinch together tightly. Repeat with the remaining dough and filling. Arrange the finished dumplings ½ inch apart in the oiled pans.

Set up a steamer and bring the water to a boil. Steam the dumplings over high heat for 10 minutes, replenishing the pot with boiling water as necessary between batches. Let the dumplings rest for a few minutes before transferring them to a serving plate. Serve hot.

VARIATIONS

✦ Use Carrot Dough (page 23), and substitute bamboo shoot filling (see page 30) for the crab filling.

✦ Use any flour dough (see page 22), and substitute mushroom filling (see page 32) for the crab filling.

BAMBOO SHOOT DUMPLINGS

Bamboo shoots are inexpensive and widely available in cans, but the piles of fresh bamboo shoots I saw in Hong Kong and Chinatown markets intrigued me. I wondered why one would go to the trouble of using fresh shoots. I decided to prepare some and was rewarded by a delightful, subtle, fresh flavor that is lost in canning. If you can find fresh shoots, start with about twice the weight you need. Peel them, cut off the tough bottoms, and parboil the shoots for 20 minutes to remove any trace of bitterness; then use as you would canned shoots.

BAMBOO SHOOT

MAKES 24 DUMPLINGS

8 to 10 dried cloud ears
2 teaspoons peanut or vegetable oil
3 ounces bamboo shoots, finely julienned
   and cut in ½-inch pieces (about ½ cup)
⅔ cup carrots, finely julienned and cut in
   ½-inch pieces
¼ cup celery, finely julienned and cut in
   ½-inch pieces
2 scallions (white and green parts), finely
   julienned and cut in ½-inch pieces
2 garlic cloves, minced
1 teaspoon soy sauce
1 teaspoon salt
2 teaspoons rice wine or dry sherry

½ teaspoon sugar
⅛ teaspoon ground white pepper
2 teaspoons cornstarch dissolved in ¼ cup
   water

Wheat Starch Dough (page 21)

Rinse the cloud ears; then soak them in hot water for 30 minutes. Cut off and discard any hard parts; then finely julienne the cloud ears. You should have about ⅓ cup.

Heat a wok or skillet, and then add the oil. When it is almost smoking, add the cloud ears, bamboo shoots, carrots, celery, scallions, and garlic and stir-fry for 2 to 3 minutes over medium heat, until the vegetables are crisp-tender. Stir in the soy sauce, salt, rice wine, sugar, and white pepper and mix well. Then add the cornstarch mixture and cook for 1 minute, or until the sauce has thickened. Let the filling cool while you make the dough.

Oil several 8- or 9-inch round cake pans.

Cut each cylinder of wheat starch dough crosswise into 8 pieces. Put one piece of dough, cut side up, between two 6-inch squares of baking parchment; then position the flat side of a cleaver blade or a flat bottom of a pan over it and press straight down to form a 3¼-inch circle. Peel off the parchment.

Spoon a heaping teaspoon of the filling onto the center of the circle of dough, leaving enough margin to pinch closed. Fold the dumpling into a semicircle and pinch the edges together tightly.

If you want to add a decorative rope border, place one corner of the folded dumpling between your thumb and knuckle of your index finger. Pinch, and then slide your thumb slightly under the newly pinched edge and roll it up toward the center at the same time you make your next pinch slightly above the first. Continue all around the semicircle. Repeat with the remaining dough and filling. Arrange the finished dumplings ½ inch apart in the oiled pans.

Set up a steamer and bring the water to a boil. Steam the dumplings over high heat for 7 minutes, replenishing the pot with boiling water as necessary between batches. Let the dumplings rest for a few minutes before transferring them to a serving plate. Serve hot.

THREE-MUSHROOM DUMPLINGS

The intense flavors of fresh and dried mushrooms make this filling one I return to often. It is excellent in wheat starch dumplings, as here, but it is versatile enough to replace meat- or seafood-based fillings in steamed, boiled, or pan-fried flour dumplings. Strict vegetarians can use vegetarian stir-fry sauce instead of oyster sauce. It's wonderful to have a frozen stash of these for appetizers, requiring only quick last-minute preparation.

MAKES 24 DUMPLINGS

6 dried shiitake mushrooms
2 teaspoons peanut or vegetable oil
6 ounces fresh white or brown
    mushrooms, finely chopped
5 ounces fresh enoki or oyster
    mushrooms, finely chopped
2 scallions (white and green parts),
    finely sliced
2 tablespoons finely chopped fresh
    cilantro
1½ teaspoons soy sauce
1 tablespoon oyster sauce or vegetarian
    stir-fry sauce
2 teaspoons rice wine or dry sherry
¼ teaspoon sugar
⅛ teaspoon ground white pepper
1 tablespoon cornstarch dissolved in
    2 tablespoons water

Wheat Starch Dough (page 21)

Put the shiitake mushrooms in a small bowl and cover with hot water. Let them stand for 30 to 45 minutes to soften. Drain the mushrooms and cut off and discard the hard stems. Rinse the caps, squeeze them dry, and chop fine.

Heat a wok or skillet; then add the oil. When it is almost smoking, add the fresh and dried mushrooms, scallions, and cilantro and stir-fry over medium heat for 4 minutes, or until most of the liquid has evaporated. Reduce the heat to low, stir in the soy sauce, oyster sauce, rice wine, sugar, and white pepper, and then add the

SHIITAKE

ENOKI

BROWN

OYSTER

M U S H R O O M S

cornstarch mixture and cook for 1 minute longer, or until the sauce has thickened. Let the filling cool before forming the dumplings. (The filling may be covered and refrigerated up to one day ahead.)

Oil several 8- or 9-inch round cake pans.

Cut each cylinder of wheat starch dough crosswise into 8 pieces. Put one piece of dough, cut side up, between two 6-inch squares of baking parchment; then position the flat side of a cleaver blade or a flat bottom of a pan over it and press straight down to form a 3¼-inch circle. Peel off the parchment.

Make a shallow pleat about ½ inch long. Make 5 or 6 more shallow pleats alongside. Your final pleat should be just over halfway around the circumference of the dough. Press a finger lightly along the inside of the pleats to flatten them slightly. Spoon a heaping teaspoon of filling into the pocket, keeping it from touching the open edge of the dough. Pinch the edges of the dough together firmly. Repeat with

the remaining dough and filling. Arrange the finished dumplings ½ inch apart in the oiled pans.

Set up a steamer and bring the water to a boil. Steam the dumplings over high heat for 7 minutes, replenishing the pot with boiling water as necessary between batches. Let the dumplings rest for a few minutes before transferring them to a serving plate. Serve hot.

VARIATIONS

✦ To make boiled dumplings with any of the flour doughs (see page 22), follow the recipe for Boiled Beef Dumplings (page 42), substituting the mushroom filling.

✦ To make potstickers with any of the flour doughs (see page 22), follow the recipe for Potstickers (page 48), substituting the mushroom filling.

PORK AND SHRIMP SIU MAI

*I have never been to a dim sum restaurant
that did not have siu mai on the menu. This
is the dumpling anyone can make, a snap with
packaged wrappers if you don't want to make
your own, and they look like far more work
than they are. Siu mai wrappers or "skins,"
also called* sue gow *wrappers, are available in
many supermarkets. A package contains about
90 wrappers; you will need only 24, but
unused wrappers may be tightly wrapped and
frozen. Thaw frozen wrappers completely
before unwrapping and using them. You may
also use wonton wrappers, either leaving them
square or cutting them into rounds with a
cookie cutter, but avoid potsticker wrappers,
which are too thick. If you cannot find packaged wrappers, this recipe includes instructions
to make your own. Make the filling first so the
dough does not rest too long.*

MAKES 24 DUMPLINGS

FILLING

8 ounces pork shoulder, coarsely
    ground or chopped
8 ounces medium shrimp, peeled,
    deveined, and cut in ½-inch
    chunks
4 water chestnuts, finely diced
1 scallion (white and green parts),
    thinly sliced
1 large egg, lightly beaten

1 teaspoon soy sauce
½ teaspoon salt
1 teaspoon rice wine or dry sherry
¼ teaspoon sugar
⅛ teaspoon ground white pepper
½ teaspoon toasted sesame oil
1 teaspoon cornstarch

DOUGH (OR USE 24 PACKAGED SIU MAI WRAPPERS)

6 tablespoons flour, plus additional for
    dusting the board
2 tablespoons plus 2 teaspoons water

GARNISH

Fresh or defrosted peas, whole fresh
    cilantro leaves, finely diced carrot, or
    finely diced red bell pepper, or a mix-
    ture totaling ¼ cup

TO MAKE THE FILLING In a medium bowl,
mix the filling ingredients together and
refrigerate for at least 30 minutes and up
to 2 hours.

Gather up edges

TO MAKE THE DOUGH In a medium bowl, mix the flour and water until combined. Turn out onto a generously floured board and knead for 3 to 4 minutes, or until smooth. The dough should be fairly stiff. Form the dough into a 9-inch cylinder, then cut it in half crosswise. Dust with flour, cover loosely with plastic wrap, and let it rest at room temperature for 20 minutes.

On a lightly floured board, use your palms to roll each cylinder out to about 12 inches. Keep the dough loosely covered with plastic wrap or an overturned bowl to prevent it from drying out. Cut each roll into 12 pieces.

TO MAKE THE DUMPLINGS Oil several 8- or 9-inch round cake pans. Roll out one piece of dough into a very thin 3-inch circle. Proceed with filling and shaping before rolling out the next piece of dough.

Put about a tablespoon of the filling onto the center of the circle of dough or packaged wrapper; then gather up the edges all around to form a cup shape. Tap the bottom lightly on a flat surface to flatten the bottom slightly. Repeat with the remaining wrappers and filling. Arrange finished dumplings ½ inch apart in the oiled pans. Garnish if desired, pressing the garnishes lightly into the filling.

Set up a steamer and bring the water to a boil. Steam the dumplings for 12 minutes over high heat, replenishing the pot with boiling water as necessary between batches. Transfer the dumplings to a serving plate. Serve hot.

PORK AND CHINESE CHIVE DUMPLINGS

We used to grow rows of Chinese chives on our farm, and they are quite different from delicate supermarket chives. Their assertive flavor gives them their other name: garlic chives. Their leaves are flat, not tubular, and they are sold in generous bunches throughout Chinatown.

See page 46 for the pan-fried chive dumplings you are more likely to find in a dim sum restaurant. This steamed version, with a generous amount of pork for body, uses chives to provide flavoring more than bulk to the filling. (Illustrated on page 16.)

MAKES 24 DUMPLINGS

Salt
4 ounces Chinese chives, cleaned,
    trimmed, and cut in ¾-inch lengths
8 ounces ground pork
1 garlic clove, finely minced
1 teaspoon soy sauce
¼ teaspoon sugar
1 teaspoon rice wine or dry sherry
1 teaspoon oyster sauce
½ teaspoon toasted sesame oil
2 teaspoons cornstarch

Wheat Starch Dough (page 21)

Combine 1 quart of water and 1 teaspoon of salt in a saucepan and bring to a boil. Add the chives and blanch for 1 minute.

Drain in a colander; then run cold water over the chives to stop the cooking, and drain again. Squeeze as much water from the chives as possible and transfer them to a medium bowl. Add the remaining filling ingredients and squeeze the mixture through your fingers to blend it well.

Oil several 8- or 9-inch round cake pans.

Cut each cylinder of wheat starch dough crosswise into 8 pieces. Press the dough between sheets of parchment to form a 3¼-inch circle. Peel off the parchment.

Spoon about 2 teaspoons of the filling onto the center of the circle of dough, leaving enough margin to pinch closed. Fold the dumpling into a semicircle and pinch the edges together tightly. Pleat the edges (see page 28).

Repeat with the remaining dough and filling. Arrange finished dumplings ½ inch apart in the oiled pans.

Set up a steamer and bring the water to a boil. Steam the dumplings over high heat for 8 minutes, replenishing the pot with boiling water as necessary between batches. Let the dumplings rest for a few minutes before transferring them to a serving plate. Serve hot.

SEAFOOD SOUP DUMPLINGS

Of all steamed dumplings, this is perhaps the most unusual and dramatic. Served in its own bowl, the large pastalike dumpling encloses a filling with a surprising ingredient: soup. This is accomplished by mixing cold, jelled chicken stock with the filling ingredients; the jelled stock liquefies when the dumpling is steamed. At one Hong Kong restaurant, the filling included threads of shark's fin, explaining why it turned out to be the most expensive item on our check. This simpler version may be enhanced with dried scallops if you want to feel extravagant. It makes a stunning, elegant first course.

Although I think it diminishes the surprise, soup dumplings are often served with additional soup ladled over them, along with a handful of colorful garnishes.

If you don't want to add soup after steaming the dumplings, omit the dried scallops, and use 2 ounces shrimp. Roll out each portion of dough into a 7-inch circle and proceed with shaping and steaming the dumplings as below. Sprinkle scallions over each bowl immediately after removing them from the steamer, and serve hot with small side dishes of either red wine or rice vinegar and thinly slivered ginger. The ginger is dipped into the vinegar and then placed on top of the dumplings as desired.

MAKES 4 INDIVIDUAL BOWLS WITH 1 DUMPLING EACH (DUMPLINGS MAY BE CUT IN HALF FOR SMALLER SERVINGS FOR 8)

Scallion

2 dried shiitake mushrooms
4 dried scallops (optional)
Scant ½ cup all-purpose flour, plus additional for dusting the board
1 large egg yolk
4 teaspoons water
3 ounces medium shrimp, peeled and deveined
3 ounces scallops, cut in ½-inch dice
2 ounces lump crabmeat, picked over for cartilage
2 ounces pork shoulder, coarsely ground or chopped
½ teaspoon salt
⅛ teaspoon ground white pepper
1 teaspoon toasted sesame oil
1 cup jelled Chicken Stock (page 39)
Peanut or vegetable oil
1 scallion (green part only), thinly sliced on the diagonal

Put the shiitake mushrooms in a small bowl and cover them with hot water. Let them stand for 30 to 45 minutes to soften. Drain the mushrooms and cut off and discard the hard stems. Rinse the caps, squeeze them dry, and cut them into thin slices. Reserve 4 slices for a garnish; then coarsely chop the remainder.

If using, place the dried scallops in a

small bowl and soak in ½ cup hot water. Let stand for 30 minutes to soften. Transfer the dried scallops and their soaking water to a small saucepan, cover, and simmer over low heat for 15 minutes, or until soft. Set aside in the cooking liquid.

In a medium bowl, combine the flour, egg yolk, and water, adding more water, a teaspoon at a time, if necessary to make a stiff dough. Turn out onto a generously floured board and knead until smooth. Dust with flour, cover loosely with plastic wrap, and let rest at room temperature for 20 minutes.

Reserve 4 shrimp, a few diced scallops, and a little crabmeat for garnish. In a medium bowl, combine the remaining shrimp, scallops, and crabmeat with the chopped mushrooms, pork, salt, white pepper, and sesame oil. Gently mix in ½ cup of the jelled chicken stock.

Oil 4 individual bowls or ramekins, each with at least a 10-ounce capacity. Divide the dough into 4 portions. Roll out one portion at a time into a 6½-inch circle. Divide the filling into 4 portions and put one portion of the filling in the center of the circle. Make small pleats all around the edge, with each pleat almost completely overlapping the previous one. The pleats will come together into a circle.

Pleat all around

Pinch center closed

Pinch closed into a point. Place the dumpling, pointed side up, in one of the oiled bowls. Repeat with the remaining dough and filling.

Set up a steamer and bring the water to a boil. Place the bowls on a steamer tier, cover, and steam for 10 minutes over high heat.

Meanwhile, place 2 cups of water in a small saucepan and bring to a boil. Add the reserved shrimp and scallops and cook for 2 to 3 minutes, or until cooked through. Drain. Heat the remaining ½ cup chicken stock in a saucepan with the reserved mushroom slices and the dried scallops with their cooking liquid. Bring to a boil. Then remove from the heat and add the shrimp, scallops, and reserved crabmeat.

Place each bowl on a plate; then ladle some soup over each portion, dividing the seafood and mushrooms evenly. Sprinkle scallions over each portion. If serving more than 4 persons, provide additional small bowls and soup spoons for each person, and small ladles at the table to split and serve the dumplings.

NOTE: If dried scallops are not used, increase the chicken stock to 1¼ cups.

heat to low, skim the stock, and simmer for 1½ hours, skimming occasionally. Strain the stock through a sieve into a clean saucepan, and discard the solids. Bring the stock to a boil; then reduce the heat to medium-low and continue cooking uncovered for 2 hours, or until the stock is reduced to 1½ to 2 cups.

Refrigerate the stock until it has set or overnight. Skim off and discard the hardened fat. Unused stock may be kept refrigerated for up to 3 days, or frozen for several months. (You may want to measure leftover stock in ½-cup portions before freezing it.) Thawed frozen stock must be reheated and then refrigerated again to jell.

CHICKEN STOCK

MAKES 1½ TO 2 CUPS

2 pounds chicken parts (such as backs, necks, wings, and bones)
1-inch piece fresh, peeled ginger, cut in half
6 whole scallions
6 cups water

In a heavy pot, combine the chicken, ginger, and scallions with 6 cups of water. Cover, bring to a boil, and then reduce the

BOILED
AND
PAN-FRIED DUMPLINGS

VEGETARIAN POTSTICKERS

Many people picture only steamed dumplings—ha gow or siu mai—when they think of dim sum, but lesser-known dumplings that are not steamed deserve a share of the limelight, too, from tender boiled ones to addictively crunchy pan-fried varieties. Include one or two recipes from this chapter in any dim sum menu; besides being rewarded with a wider variety of flavors and textures, the cook will appreciate being able to pan-fry or boil some dumplings while the steamer is going rather than having to juggle four or five steamed varieties at once.

Of course, these dumplings have virtues all their own, aside from pragmatic considerations. When flour dough dumplings are boiled instead of steamed, they become silkier and more pastalike, akin to wonton. (Note that pan-fried flour dough dumplings such as potstickers may be boiled rather than fried for a simpler, lower-fat version.)

You won't find them on dim sum carts, but I also like boiled dumplings served in a bowl like wonton, perhaps on a bed of boiled noodles with a ladleful of chicken broth, a scattering of slivered scallions, a squirt of toasted sesame oil, and a few drops of soy sauce or oyster sauce. Freeze some uncooked dumplings and you'll always have the makings of a quick, light supper on hand.

Pan-frying brings out the fragrance of the filling within dumplings and adds a crisp dimension to the chewiness of their wrappers. Both wheat starch dumplings and flour dough dumplings are cooked the same way: The dumplings are briefly pan-fried in a small amount of oil; then water is added and allowed to boil away and finish cooking the dough. The dumplings continue cooking until the bottoms are crisp and brown. Wheat starch dough will become translucent and chewy, while the flour dough will become pastalike with a more pronounced crisp bottom.

WIRE MESH STRAINER

BOILED BEEF DUMPLINGS

I can rarely resist these beef dumplings on a cart; the beef filling provides a welcome contrast to the ubiquitous pork varieties. Serve these with a dipping sauce spiked with a little vinegar. You may also cook these like Potstickers (page 48).

MAKES 24 DUMPLINGS

FILLING

10 ounces lean ground beef
1 scallion (white and green parts), thinly
   sliced
1½ teaspoons soy sauce
1 teaspoon salt
1 teaspoon rice wine or dry sherry
½ teaspoon sugar
⅛ teaspoon ground white pepper
1 teaspoon toasted sesame oil
2 teaspoons cornstarch

Flour Dough (page 22) or 24 packaged
   potsticker wrappers
Soy Vinegar Dip (page 136)

In a medium bowl, mix all the filling ingredients together, squeezing the mixture through your fingers to blend it well. Divide the mixture into 4 portions, and then form each portion into 6 balls. Cover and refrigerate for at least 30 minutes and up to 2 hours.

Press to seal

Line a baking sheet with parchment and dust lightly with flour.

Cut each cylinder of dough into 12 pieces. On a floured board, use a rolling pin to roll one piece to a 3¼-inch circle. Make a pleat along the edge ¼ inch wide by ½ inch long. Make a second pleat facing toward the first, so the pleated edges touch. Make one more pleat to the outside of each of these pleats, also facing inward. Fill with one portion of the beef. If using packaged wrappers, dip a finger in water and run it all around the inside edge. Press the unpleated edge to the pleated edge to seal. Repeat with the remaining dough and filling. Place the dumplings on the baking sheet and cover loosely with plastic

wrap. (At this point, the dumplings may be frozen until firm, about 45 minutes, and then transferred to a plastic bag and sealed tightly.)

Bring 4 quarts of water to a boil in a large pot. Drop the dumplings quickly one by one into the water, stirring them gently to separate. Return to a boil; then reduce the heat to medium and cook for 6 to 7 minutes (1 to 2 minutes longer if frozen), or until the dumplings float to the top and the filling is cooked through. Scoop out the dumplings with a wire strainer or slotted spoon, shake off the water, and arrange the dumplings on a platter. Serve hot with soy vinegar dip.

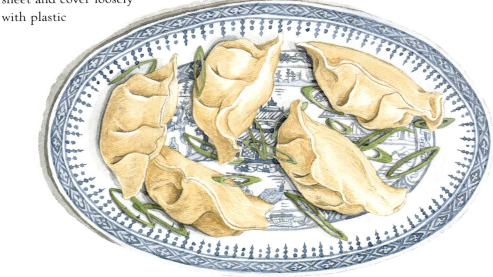

FISH DUMPLINGS

One of my all-time favorite dishes is steamed fish the way my mother and grandparents made it; simply dressed with ginger, scallions, oil, and soy sauce, the pure, sweet fish flavor shines through. Here's a way to capture that in tender green boiled dumplings strewn with slivers of ginger and scallions.

MAKES 24 DUMPLINGS

FILLING

10 ounces snapper or cod fillet, coarsely ground or chopped
2 teaspoons minced peeled fresh ginger
1 scallion (white and green parts), minced
1 teaspoon soy sauce
½ teaspoon salt
1 teaspoon rice wine or dry sherry
1 teaspoon peanut or vegetable oil
1 teaspoon cornstarch

Spinach Dough (page 22) or 24 packaged siu mai or potsticker wrappers (see Note)

1 tablespoon peanut or vegetable oil
½-inch piece fresh ginger, peeled and cut into fine slivers
1 tablespoon scallion (green part only), finely sliced on the diagonal
1 tablespoon soy sauce

Mix the filling ingredients together until well blended. Refrigerate for at least 30 minutes and up to 2 hours.

Line a baking sheet with parchment and dust lightly with flour.

Cut each cylinder of spinach dough into 12 pieces. On a floured board, use a rolling pin to roll one piece to a 3¼-inch circle. Spoon a heaping teaspoon of the filling onto the center of the circle of dough, leaving enough margin to pinch closed. If using packaged wrappers, dip a finger in water and run it all around the top edge. Fold the dumpling into a semicircle and pinch the edges together tightly. With the flat side up, folded edge toward you, draw the corners toward you and pinch them together to form a circular shape. Repeat with the remaining dough and filling.

Place the dumplings on the baking sheet, and cover loosely with plastic wrap. (At this point, the dumplings may be frozen until firm, about 45 minutes, and then transferred to a plastic bag and sealed tightly.)

Bring 4 quarts of water to a boil in a large pot. Drop the dumplings quickly one by one into the water, stirring gently to separate. Return to a boil, then reduce the

heat to medium and cook for 4 to
5 minutes (1 to 2 minutes longer if
frozen), or until the dumplings float
to the top and the filling is cooked
through. Scoop out the dumplings
with a wire strainer or slotted spoon,
shake off the water, and arrange the
dumplings on a platter.

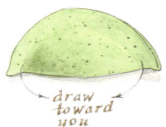

*draw
toward
you*

pinch together

Meanwhile, heat a small skillet,
and then add the oil. When it is almost
smoking, add the ginger and scallion and
stir-fry for 1 minute. Remove from the
heat and stir in the soy sauce.

Drizzle the mixture over the finished
dumplings. Serve hot.

NOTE: Potsticker wrappers are sturdier,
but more delicate siu mai wrappers are a
better match for the fish filling.

VARIATION

The fish filling can be used to make
20 to 24 siu mai, using either packaged siu mai wrappers or a half-
recipe of spinach dough, rolling out
the dough into very thin 3-inch circles.
Shape and steam as for Pork and Shrimp
Siu Mai (page 34). Serve the soy sauce
mixture as a dipping sauce.

FISH DUMPLINGS

CHINESE CHIVE DUMPLINGS

Flat-leaved Chinese chives, also called garlic chives, are the main ingredient rather than an accent in these dumplings. The dumplings are always recognizable by the emerald hue of the filling shining through and the crisp pan-fried spot on top. The slightly crisp pan-fried crust is a perfect match for the garlicky chive flavor. Do not substitute common tubular-leaved chives because they can taste bitter in such quantity.

These dumplings brown better when they are pan-fried in a pan that does not have a nonstick coating. Also, note that these dumplings do not freeze well.

MAKES ABOUT 18 DUMPLINGS

1½ teaspoons salt
½ pound Chinese chives, cleaned, trimmed, and cut in ½-inch lengths
4 ounces shrimp, peeled, deveined, and cut in ¼-inch dice (about ½ cup)
½ teaspoon soy sauce
⅛ teaspoon ground white pepper
½ teaspoon toasted sesame oil
1 teaspoon cornstarch

Wheat Starch Dough, substituting 1 tablespoon glutinous rice flour for 1 tablespoon of the tapioca flour (page 21)
Peanut or vegetable oil, for pan-frying

Bring 2 quarts of water and 1 teaspoon of the salt to a boil in a large saucepan. Add the chives and blanch for 1 minute over high heat. Drain the chives in a colander, and rinse under cold water to stop the cooking. Squeeze the chives dry and transfer them to a medium bowl. (You should have about 1¼ cups.)

Preheat the oven to 200°F.

Combine the chives with the remaining ½ teaspoon salt, the shrimp, soy sauce, white pepper, sesame oil, and cornstarch. Set aside.

Cut each cylinder of wheat starch

about 2 inches

dough crosswise into 6 pieces. Put one piece of dough, cut side up, between two 6-inch squares of baking parchment; then position the flat side of a cleaver blade or a flat bottom of a pan over it and press straight down to form a 3½-inch circle. Peel off the parchment.

Spoon about 2 teaspoons of the filling onto the center of a circle. Make 8 to 10 pleats all around the edge, bringing up the sides evenly, and then pinch closed. Turn the dumpling pinched side down, and pat it gently to flatten it into a 2-inch disk. Repeat with the remaining dough and filling. Lightly dust a board with wheat starch; then place the finished dumplings on it.

Heat a large skillet over medium-high heat, and then add 1 tablespoon oil. When it is almost smoking, arrange one layer of dumplings in the skillet, leaving enough room so they are not touching one another. (You will have to cook the dumplings in 2 or 3 batches.) Cook the dumplings for 2 to 3 minutes on each side, pressing them gently with a spatula, until they turn crisp and just begin to brown. Carefully add ½ cup water (it will spatter), cover the skillet tightly, reduce the heat to low, and cook for 3 minutes, or until the dough becomes somewhat translucent around the sides. Uncover, raise the heat to medium, and cook for 3 to 4 minutes longer, or until the water has evaporated; turn the dumplings to cook until both sides become slightly crisp and light brown. Transfer the dumplings to a serving plate, cover them lightly with foil, and keep them warm in the oven while you make the next batches. Serve hot.

VARIATION

Omit the shrimp and substitute one of the following: 4 ounces ground pork or chicken, or 1 medium boiled potato, peeled and cut in ¼-inch dice (about ½ cup).

POTSTICKERS

Friends unfamiliar with dim sum have some-times accompanied me to a restaurant with trepidation, but not one has been able to resist a good, crisp potsticker. According to legend, potstickers were created when a cook panicked and poured water over some dumplings that were beginning to burn. With nothing else to offer, he served them anyway, and they were such a success they've been cooked that way ever since.

The most common filling for potstickers is a ground pork and napa cabbage mixture sea-soned with ginger and toasted sesame oil; the flavors blend so well it's no wonder they are a teahouse favorite. If you cannot find napa cab-bage, you may substitute green cabbage, although it does not have as fine a texture. Potsticker filling variations include a vegetarian version with tofu standing in for the meat, and a fragrant curried version that can use pork, chicken, or tofu as its main ingredient.

MAKES 24 POTSTICKERS

8 ounces finely shredded napa cabbage
    (about 3 cups)
1 tablespoon salt
8 ounces ground pork
2 tablespoons crushed or finely minced
    peeled fresh ginger
1 scallion (white and green parts), finely
    sliced

2 teaspoons soy sauce
2 teaspoons rice wine
½ teaspoon sugar
1 tablespoon toasted sesame oil

Flour Dough, any variation (page 22),
    or 24 packaged potsticker wrappers
    (see Note)
Soy Vinegar Dip (page 136)
2 tablespoons peanut or vegetable oil

In a large bowl, toss the napa cabbage with the salt and let stand for 30 minutes, until wilted. Rinse the cabbage, and then squeeze out as much water as possible. You should have about 2 cups of cabbage.

Preheat the oven to 200°F.

In a bowl, mix the pork, ginger, scal-lion, soy sauce, rice wine, sugar, and sesame oil, squeezing the mixture through your fingers to blend it well. Mix in the cabbage. Refrigerate the filling for at least 20 minutes and up to 2 hours.

Cut each cylinder of dough into 12 pieces. On a floured board, use a rolling pin to roll one piece to a 3¼-inch circle. Make a pleat along the edge ¼ inch wide by ½ inch long (see page 51). Make 3 more pleats alongside, with the first pleat being hindmost. Fill with about a table-spoon of the filling. If using packaged wrappers, dip a finger in water and run it all around the inside edge. Press the unpleated edge to the pleated edge to seal. Repeat with the remaining dough and filling. Set the finished potstickers on a well-floured baking sheet.

Heat a skillet; then add 1 tablespoon of the oil. When it is almost smoking, arrange half the potstickers in the skillet as close to one another as possible without letting them touch. Pan-fry for 2 to 3 minutes over medium heat, checking frequently to make sure they are not burning. Reduce the heat if they are browning too quickly; packaged wrappers will brown more quickly than homemade wrappers.

Carefully pour ½ cup of water into the skillet. The water may spatter, so add a little, stand back, and then add the rest. Cover, reduce the heat to low, and simmer for 5 to 6 minutes, or until most of the water has evaporated. If it is evaporating too fast, add 1 to 2 tablespoons of water to give the filling enough time to cook through. Uncover, raise the heat to medium-high, and cook for 2 to 3 minutes longer, or until all the water has evaporated and the bottoms of the potstickers are brown and crisp. With a spatula, transfer the potstickers, browned side up, to a

serving plate. Keep the potstickers warm in the oven while making the second batch. Serve hot with soy vinegar dip.

NOTE: Homemade wrappers will form a more substantial, crisper bottom than packaged wrappers. A package of potsticker wrappers should contain about forty to sixty 3-inch round wrappers. Do not substitute siu mai, sue gow, or wonton wrappers, which are too thin to pan-fry.

PORK and CABBAGE POTSTICKERS

VARIATIONS
CURRIED POTSTICKER FILLING

The curry flavor in this potsticker filling is robust enough to make dipping sauce unnecessary. Curry dough makes beautiful golden dumplings and amplifies the flavors even more.

2 teaspoons peanut or vegetable oil
⅓ cup finely chopped onion
¼ cup finely diced carrot
8 ounces boneless, skinless chicken (mixture of light and dark meat), or pork, cut in ¼-inch dice, or 6 ounces tofu, cut in ¼-inch dice, then slightly mashed
¼ cup peas, fresh or defrosted
1½ teaspoons curry powder
1½ teaspoons salt
2 teaspoons rice wine or dry sherry
½ teaspoon sugar
1 teaspoon cornstarch

Heat a skillet, and then add the oil. When it is almost smoking, add the onion and carrot and stir-fry over medium heat for about 3 minutes, or until the onion is translucent. Transfer the mixture to a medium bowl and let it cool. Mix in the chicken, peas, curry powder, salt, rice wine, sugar, and cornstarch. Proceed as on page 48.

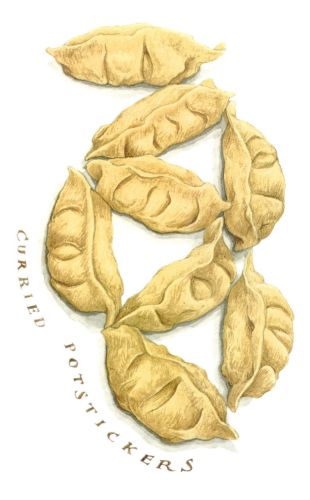

CURRIED POTSTICKERS

Press to seal

VEGETARIAN POTSTICKER FILLING

For the vegetarian potsticker fan, tofu replaces pork in this filling; shredded cloud ears add color and texture. (Illustrated on page 40.)

8 ounces finely shredded napa cabbage
   (about 3 cups)
1 tablespoon salt
3 scallions (white and green parts), thinly
   sliced
2 tablespoons crushed or finely minced
   peeled fresh ginger
4 ounces firm tofu, mashed
½ ounce (dry weight) cloud ears, soaked,
   drained, and finely shredded (optional)
2 teaspoons soy sauce
2 teaspoons toasted sesame oil
2 teaspoons rice wine or dry sherry
⅛ teaspoon ground white pepper

Soy Vinegar Dip (page 136)

In a large bowl, toss the napa cabbage with the salt and let stand for 30 minutes, until wilted. Rinse the cabbage; then squeeze out as much water as possible. You should have about 2 cups of cabbage.

   In a bowl, mix the cabbage with the scallions, ginger, tofu, cloud ears, soy sauce, sesame oil, rice wine, and white pepper. Proceed as on page 48. Serve hot with soy vinegar dip.

BREADS
AND
BAKED
DISHES

Originating in northern China, breads are a dim sum staple. They are almost always filled, and they may be baked, pan-fried, or steamed, for very different appearances. The soft white dough of a steamed bun splits open to reveal bits of its char siu filling as it cooks, while baked buns shine with a golden egg glaze. The pleated, twisted tops of pan-fried buns are dipped in scallions, and they release their fragrance as they brown.

Pancakes range from the sturdy scallion-filled staple, coiled and flattened to make a dense, chewy bread, to tender, crepelike filled pancakes wrapped around seasoned greens and pan-fried to a delicate crispness.

Savory pastries are favorite baked dim sum choices. Interleaved doughs puff up into rich, flaky layers surrounding a bite of char siu or curried filling.

STEAMED BAO DOUGH

On a dim sum menu, bao—or bread—almost
always means steamed, white, cakelike buns
filled with either a savory meat mixture or a
sweetened paste made from lotus seeds or
beans.

 Moist heat, low-gluten cake flour, and the
unusual combination of yeast with baking powder, baking soda, and vinegar contribute to their
lightness; a cheesecloth lining in the steamer
and a bit of shortening in the dough keep the
buns from becoming soggy. If you are using a
pot for a steamer, substitute a cheesecloth-lined,
collapsible, perforated vegetable steamer for the
usual stand and heatproof dish, because steam
must circulate under the buns.

DOUGH FOR 24 BUNS

STARTER

2 teaspoons active dry yeast
1 cup lukewarm water
½ cup sugar
1½ cups cake flour

DOUGH

½ teaspoon salt
1 tablespoon rice vinegar
2 cups cake flour, plus about ¼ cup
 additional for dusting the board
1 tablespoon baking powder
¼ teaspoon baking soda
1 tablespoon vegetable shortening

TO MAKE THE STARTER In a large bowl, mix
the yeast with the lukewarm water and sugar
and let the mixture stand for 10 minutes.
Stir in the cake flour until well blended.
Cover the bowl with plastic wrap and let the
mixture rise in a warm, draft-free place for
1 hour, or until puffed and bubbly.

TO MAKE THE DOUGH Stir the salt and
vinegar into the starter. In another bowl,
sift together the 2 cups cake flour, baking
powder, and baking soda. Stir the flour
mixture into the yeast mixture. When
combined, add the shortening and work it
in with your fingers. The dough will
become a sticky, somewhat shaggy mass.
Turn the dough out onto a well-floured
board and knead it for about 5 minutes, or
until smooth, adding flour as necessary.
Grease a clean, large bowl with a little
shortening, place the dough in the bowl,
and cover it with a damp cloth or plastic
wrap. Let it rise in a warm, draft-free place
for 1 hour. (If you have made a bao filling
ahead and refrigerated it, take it out now
to let it come back to room temperature.)

 Lightly punch the dough down, and
then proceed as directed for Steamed
Char Siu Bao (page 54) or Steamed Sweet
Bao (page 124).

STEAMED CHAR SIU BAO

Classmates used to look askance when I unpacked one of these white buns from my school lunch box; they appeared uncooked—not nicely browned like a familiar biscuit or brown-and-serve roll. More daring friends would take up my offer of a bite and be rewarded with a taste of steamed bread, bursting with cubes of Chinese roasted pork—char siu—in a richly flavored sauce.

Char siu bao is a dim sum standard. If you aren't near a Chinatown deli, see page 114 for making your own char siu. Cooled buns may be sealed in a plastic bag, and either refrigerated for several days or frozen for up to a month. Thaw the buns before reheating them; then steam them for 5 to 6 minutes over boiling water.

MAKES 24 BUNS

FILLING
1 tablespoon sugar
2 teaspoons soy sauce
1 teaspoon rice wine or dry sherry
1 tablespoon oyster sauce
1 tablespoon hoisin sauce
1 teaspoon toasted sesame oil
1 tablespoon cornstarch dissolved in
    1 tablespoon water
½ pound char siu, cut into ½-inch dice

Steamed Bao Dough (page 53)

In a small saucepan, mix together ⅓ cup water, the sugar, soy sauce, rice wine, oyster sauce, hoisin sauce, and sesame oil. Cook the sauce over medium heat until it is bubbly. Stir in the cornstarch mixture and cook for about 1 minute, or until the sauce has thickened. Remove the sauce from the heat and stir in the diced char siu. Cool to room temperature. (The filling may be covered and refrigerated a day ahead. Allow the filling to reach room temperature before using.)

CHAR SIU BAO

Line a steamer basket (see page 17) or metal steamer tiers with several layers of dampened cheesecloth. Cut twenty-four 2-inch squares of baking parchment.

Divide the dough into 24 pieces. Use your fingertips to flatten one piece lightly into a 3-inch circle. Place the circle flat on one palm. Spoon about 2 teaspoons of the filling onto the center. Then gather the edges of the dough together and pinch tightly. Place the bun pinched side up on a square of parchment, and place it in a prepared steamer tier. Repeat with the remaining dough and filling, spacing the buns 1 inch apart on the steamer tiers. Stack the tiers (excluding the steamer bottom), covering the top tier loosely with plastic wrap. Let the buns rise for 30 minutes. You will have to steam the buns in 2 or 3 batches.

Bring the water in the steamer to a boil over high heat. Steam a single tier of buns at a time over high heat for 12 minutes, replenishing the pot with water as necessary between batches. Serve hot.

VARIATION
VEGETARIAN "CHAR SIU" BAO

Substitute 1 tablespoon vegetarian stir-fry sauce for the oyster sauce. Substitute ½ cup onion, finely chopped, and 10 ounces firm tofu, cut into ½-inch dice, for the char siu.

Combine ⅓ cup water, the sugar, soy sauce, rice wine, vegetarian stir-fry sauce, hoisin sauce, and sesame oil in a small bowl and set aside. Heat a nonstick skillet over medium heat; then add 2 teaspoons peanut oil. When it is almost smoking, add the onion and stir-fry for 2 minutes, until transparent. Add the tofu and stir-fry for 2 to 3 minutes longer, or until the tofu is lightly browned. Add the sauce mixture and cook it for 30 seconds, or until it is bubbly. Add the cornstarch mixture and cook, stirring constantly, for about 1 minute longer, or until the sauce has thickened. Remove the filling from the heat and cool to room temperature.

You may want to mash a small amount of the tofu before stirring it into the filling. The filling may be covered and refrigerated up to a day ahead. Proceed as above.

PAN-FRIED BAO

Pan-frying and then simmering these buns produces the browned crust of a baked bun and the tenderness of a steamed bun. I anticipated extensive trial and error would be needed to perfect this recipe, but the very first try yielded such good results I had to restrain myself from eating half of them in one sitting. The soft dough is a perfect foil for many fillings; you could substitute those used for Potstickers (page 48), or for Pork and Chinese Chive Dumplings (page 36). With the latter, beef may be substituted for the pork if you like. A nonstick skillet works best with this dish, and it must have a tight-fitting lid.

MAKES 24 BUNS

Steamed Bao Dough (page 53)

FILLING
4 ounces spinach leaves
8 ounces ground pork or boneless, skinless chicken (mixture of light and dark meat), coarsely ground
1 scallion (white and green parts), thinly sliced
1 tablespoon finely chopped fresh cilantro
1 teaspoon soy sauce
½ teaspoon salt
1 teaspoon rice wine or dry sherry
¼ teaspoon sugar
1 teaspoon toasted sesame oil
⅛ teaspoon ground white pepper

1 tablespoon all-purpose flour mixed with 2 tablespoons water

¼ cup minced scallions (white and green parts), or minced fresh cilantro leaves, for garnish
Peanut or vegetable oil, for pan-frying

Make the dough and let it rise while making the filling.

Wash the spinach and shake off most of the water. Put the spinach in a dry saucepan, cover, and cook over medium-low heat for 2 to 3 minutes, turning the leaves over occasionally, until the spinach is wilted but still bright green. Transfer the spinach to a plate and let it cool. Squeeze the spinach to remove as much water as possible; then chop it fine.

In a bowl, combine the spinach with the remaining filling ingredients. Squeeze the filling between your fingers to blend it well. Divide the filling into 4 portions; then divide each portion into 6 balls. Cover and refrigerate.

Divide the dough into 24 pieces. Roll out one piece into a 3½-inch circle, thinner around the outside than at the center. Place one portion of the filling onto the center; then pinch small pleats all around (see page 47) to enclose the filling completely. Twist the top closed. Dip the top into the flour mixture, and then dip it into the minced scallions or cilantro. Space the buns, pinched side up, 1 inch apart on a well-floured surface. Cover loosely with plastic wrap and let the buns rise for 30 minutes.

Heat a nonstick skillet over medium heat; then add 1 tablespoon oil. When it is almost smoking, arrange a layer of buns, pinched side up, ½ inch apart in the skillet. Cook for 2 to 3 minutes, or until the bottoms of the buns are golden brown. Watch the buns carefully and reduce the heat if they are browning too quickly. Carefully pour ½ cup water into the skillet, and cover it tightly. Cook for 5 to 6 minutes, or until almost the water has evaporated. Uncover, and continue cooking until the water has completely evaporated and the bottoms of the buns are crisp. Flip the buns over, pressing on them slightly with the back of a spatula, and cook them for about 1 minute longer, until the tops are slightly browned. Repeat with the remaining buns, adding more oil to the skillet as needed.

Serve hot.

PAN-FRIED BAO

BAKED CHAR SIU BAO

Besides the white steamed bao, the other ubiquitous buns on dim sum carts are these golden domes. When making your own, the soft egg-glazed buns and savory char siu filling fill the kitchen with their mouthwatering aroma. If twenty-four seems like too many to make, remember these freeze well and reheat beautifully. You can make and refrigerate the filling up to 2 days before making the dough. The dough is also used for Baked Sweet Bao (page 123).

San Francisco was the edge of my universe when I was young. In my fantasies, it was the place I would go when I ran away from home. I had no idea where I'd stay, but food was covered: I could go to my favorite

Grant Avenue bakery, where for seventy-five cents a day, I could buy three of their enormous baked char siu bao—one for every meal. At one point I had enough saved up for two weeks—surely long enough to be begged to return home.

MAKES TWENTY-FOUR 3-INCH BUNS

DOUGH

3¼ to 3½ cups all-purpose flour, plus
    additional for dusting the board
½ teaspoon salt
¼ cup sugar
¼ cup vegetable shortening
¼ cup plus ⅓ cup lukewarm water, divided
1½ teaspoons active dry yeast
1 cup milk

Peanut or vegetable oil, for the baking
    sheets
Char Siu Bao filling (see page 54), at room
    temperature
1 large egg, beaten

Sift 2 cups of the flour, the salt, and sugar into a large bowl. With a pastry blender or two knives, cut in the shortening until the flour resembles coarse meal.

In a small bowl, mix ¼ cup of the lukewarm water with the yeast and let it soften for 5 minutes.

Put the milk and the remaining ⅓ cup

water in a medium saucepan and heat the mixture to 110°F. Remove the pan from the heat, and stir in the yeast mixture. Add the yeast and milk to the flour mixture, and mix well.

Add the remaining 1¼ to 1½ cups of flour, and mix until the dough becomes a sticky, somewhat shaggy mass. Turn the dough out onto a well-floured board. Knead for 5 to 8 minutes, or until the dough is smooth and elastic, adding flour to the board as necessary to keep the dough from sticking.

Grease a clean, large bowl with shortening. Place the dough in the bowl and turn it to coat all sides. Cover the bowl with plastic wrap, and let the dough rise in a warm, draft-free place for 2 hours, until doubled in bulk.

Oil 2 baking sheets and set them aside.

Punch down the risen dough, and turn it out onto a well-floured board. Pat the dough into an 8 × 12-inch rectangle; then cut it into 24 equal portions, each about 2 inches square.

Hold a portion of dough on one palm and flatten it with your fingers into a 2½-inch circle, slightly thicker in the middle than around the edges. Place a heaping teaspoon of the filling onto the center. Gather the edges of the dough together and pinch firmly to seal in the filling completely.

Put the bun, pinched side down, on the oiled baking sheet. Repeat with the remaining ingredients, spacing finished buns 2 inches apart. Cover the buns loosely with plastic wrap, and let them rise in a warm, draft-free place for 30 minutes.

Preheat the oven to 350°F.

With a pastry brush, brush the buns lightly with the beaten egg.

Bake the buns for 20 to 25 minutes, until golden brown. To check for doneness, tear a bun in half; the bread should be airy rather than raw-looking and doughy.

Transfer the buns to a wire rack to cool slightly before serving.

Once they have cooled completely, the buns may be covered and refrigerated for up to 24 hours. Let the buns reach room temperature; then reheat them for 5 to 7 minutes in a 350°F. oven, or until they are heated through.

These buns also freeze well. Let them thaw completely, and then reheat as above.

SCALLION PANCAKES

Hot out of the skillet, these dense, chewy pan-cakes tease the appetite with their fragrant scal-lions and a generous sprinkling of salt. I also sampled a version of these in Hong Kong that were rolled up into small rings and deep-fried, but the larger pan-fried pancakes are both eas-ier to make and more typical. They make an especially good appetizer.

MAKES 6 PANCAKES, EACH CUT IN 4 TO 6 WEDGES

1½ cups all-purpose flour, plus additional
    for dusting the board
½ cup boiling water
2 tablespoons cold water
4 to 6 scallions (white and green parts),
    thinly sliced (about 1 cup)
1 tablespoon vegetable shortening
Salt
2 to 4 tablespoons peanut or vegetable oil

Sift the flour into a large bowl. Stir in the boiling water until well blended; then add the cold water. Knead the dough on a lightly floured surface for 4 to 5 minutes, or until the dough is firm and elastic. Form the dough into a ball, dust it with flour, wrap it with plastic wrap, and let it rest on the surface for 30 minutes.

    Preheat the oven to 200°F. Cover a baking sheet with several layers of paper towels and set it aside.

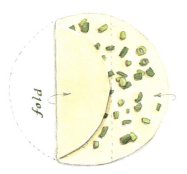

Fold

7 inches

Roll

Stand on end

Flatten

5 inches

Divide the scallions into 6 equal portions. Divide the dough into 6 pieces. On a lightly floured surface, roll out one piece of dough into a 7½-inch circle. Spread ½ teaspoon shortening on the dough to within ¼ inch of the edge. Sprinkle the dough with a scant ¼ teaspoon salt and one portion of the scallions; then lightly press the salt and scallions into the dough. Fold the dough in thirds, pinch the ends closed, and roll the dough up loosely from one short end like a jelly roll. Turn the coil round side up, dust a little flour on it, flatten it slightly with your fingers, and roll it into a 5-inch circle. Repeat with the remaining dough and filling ingredients.

Heat a nonstick skillet over medium heat; then add 1 teaspoon oil. When it is almost smoking, place one pancake in the skillet, and cook it for 2 to 3 minutes on each side, turning it once, until golden brown. Add another teaspoon of oil to the skillet when you turn the pancake. Lift an edge of the pancake occasionally to check for overbrowning and reduce the heat if necessary. Transfer the pancake to the baking sheet and keep it warm in the oven while cooking the remaining pancakes. Add oil to the skillet for each pancake. Cut each pancake into 4 to 6 wedges. Serve hot.

VARIATION

Spread ½ teaspoon toasted sesame oil instead of shortening on each circle of dough.

SAVORY FILLED PANCAKES

These colorful, tender pancakes may be assembled ahead and pan-fried just before serving. Choose tender pea shoots with a minimum of curled tendrils. The pancakes are also used with Sweet Red-Bean Filling (page 125).

MAKES 4 PANCAKES, EACH CUT IN 6 PIECES

8 ounces pea shoots
Salt
3 tablespoons peanut or vegetable oil, plus
    additional if needed
2 garlic cloves, finely minced
4 ounces shrimp, peeled, deveined, and cut
    into ½-inch chunks
1 teaspoon soy sauce
2 teaspoons toasted sesame oil
4 pancakes, unfilled (see page 130)
1 tablespoon flour mixed with
    1 tablespoon water

Rinse and drain the pea shoots. Pinch off and discard any thick, tough stems or long, curled tendrils. Add 1 teaspoon of salt to 3 quarts of water in a large pot and bring to a boil. Blanch the pea shoots for 2 minutes in the boiling water. Taste for doneness; they should have a pleasant crunch, but not be overly chewy. Drain the pea shoots in a colander, rinse them under cold water to stop the cooking, drain again, and then squeeze them dry. Chop them coarse.

Heat a skillet over medium heat; then add 1 tablespoon peanut oil. When it is almost smoking, add the garlic, reduce the heat to low, and stir-fry for 1 minute. Add the shrimp, raise the heat to medium and cook for about 1½ minutes, until the shrimp are cooked through. Do not let the garlic brown or it will become bitter. Remove the mixture from the heat, add the soy sauce, ½ teaspoon salt, sesame oil, and chopped pea shoots, and toss to mix the ingredients well. Set aside to cool.

Divide the filling into 4 portions. Spread one portion down the length of each pancake, just left of the center (see page 131). Dab a little flour mixture around the edge to the right of the center. Roll the pancake, starting from the left, to make a flattened cylinder. Press the edge lightly to seal in the filling.

Heat the skillet over medium-high heat, and then add the remaining 2 tablespoons of peanut oil. When it is almost smoking, cook 1 or 2 filled pancakes at a time for 1 to 2 minutes, until browned; then turn them over and cook 1 to 2 minutes longer to brown the other side, adding oil as necessary.

Place several layers of paper towels on a plate. Drain the pancakes on the paper towels while you cook the remaining pancakes. Transfer the pancakes to a serving plate; then cut each pancake crosswise into 4 to 6 pieces. Serve hot.

VARIATIONS

✦ Omit the pea shoots, and substitute 1 pound spinach, washed, stemmed, and cooked until just wilted. Cool the spinach to room temperature, squeeze out excess liquid, and chop the spinach fine.

✦ Omit the shrimp, and substitute 4 ounces char siu, cut in matchsticks. Add the char siu with the soy sauce, salt, and sesame oil.

FLAKY PASTRY DOUGH

This multilayered dough is used to make Char Siu Pastries (page 66) and Savory Turnovers (page 68). It is actually two doughs—one a water dough, the other a delicate short dough—folded together and rolled out like puff pastry dough. You can form it into one large sheet to cut into rectangular pastries, or roll it out into small circles to shape into turnovers. Although I generally use vegetable shortening instead of lard, I have to admit the pastries made with lard taste superior.

The dough may be started a day ahead, so that the final assembly and baking are fairly quick, simple procedures. Unbaked pastries also freeze beautifully.

MAKES DOUGH FOR 12 PASTRIES

WATER DOUGH
1 cup all-purpose flour, plus additional for
　　dusting the board
1 teaspoon sugar
¼ cup vegetable shortening or lard
Ice water

SHORT DOUGH
½ cup all-purpose flour
⅓ cup vegetable shortening or lard

TO MAKE THE WATER DOUGH Combine 1 cup flour with the sugar. Cut in the shortening with a pastry blender or two knives until the mixture resembles coarse bread crumbs. With a fork, stir in ¼ cup ice water; then add 1 teaspoon ice water at a time as necessary, until all of the flour has been moistened and the dough is a shaggy mass. Turn the dough out onto a floured board and knead it briefly until it just holds together in a ball. Wrap the dough in plastic wrap, and then roll the dough through the plastic wrap to form a rectangle measuring 5 × 8½ inches (for char siu pastries) or 4 × 6 inches (for savory turnovers). Refrigerate the dough for at least 1 hour.

TO MAKE THE SHORT DOUGH Place the flour in a medium bowl. Cut in the shortening with a pastry blender or two knives until it has the texture of coarse meal. Wrap the dough in plastic wrap, and then shape the dough through the plastic wrap to form a 3 × 4-inch rectangle. Refrigerate the dough for at least 1 hour; then roll and shape the dough as directed in the following recipes.

A TRIP TO THE LUK YU TEA HOUSE

So much has been written about the Luk Yu Tea House that it was at the top of my list when my husband and I decided to explore dim sum in Hong Kong. In existence since the 1930s, it has operated at its present location for more than twenty-five years.

Research had warned us to arrive early to avoid long waits. We also read that well before noon, the tray-laden waitresses would disappear and we would have to order by circling our selections from a pad of Chinese-only menus; help deciphering would not necessarily be forthcoming.

I don't know what I expected—a tourist trap, alarming chaos—but we arrived so early that we immediately garnered a booth in the half-empty room. Memories of my grandfather's restaurant overpowered me, perhaps triggered by the dark wood chairs measured long ago for smaller bodies, or the shuffle of a waiter's feet as he hauled a battered kettle from table to table, refilling teapots with boiling water. This place was more elegant than what I had known growing up, but it was worn enough to feel somehow familiar.

Some of the waitresses were so old I felt as if I were rudely making my grandmother serve me. Other little touches betrayed the restaurant's age. Waitresses bore highly polished but battered metal trays instead of plastic ones, and the few trolleys looked as if they had traveled many miles. Bamboo steamers were lined with cut bamboo leaves instead of stamped-out parchment circles. An oft-mentioned brass spittoon rested at the foot of our table.

And the food! It was perhaps not the most innovative selection we came across, but everything we ordered tasted as if the recipe had been perfected long ago, and followed with care ever since. One dish I had to have was steamed bao. Restaurants usually offer three bao to a plate, or at least two, but here a single bun covered the entire plate. Inside, it was stuffed with a delectable mixture of preserved egg, chicken, and char siu, and the bread was light, fluffy, and perfectly steamed. It was impossible to finish; the bao was an ample meal in itself.

We ordered too much, of course. Only a long afternoon of elbowing through Hong Kong crowds could revive our sated appetites and make us wish we had packed up those last morsels of our Luk Yu feast.

CHAR SIU PASTRIES

In the name of research, I ordered these char siu soo in Hong Kong, Vancouver, and San Francisco whenever I saw them. I cannot say I was ever disappointed. Fresh out of the oven, they are impossible to resist, with a flaky crust that all but falls apart around a mouthful of intensely flavorful filling.

MAKES 12 PASTRIES

Flaky Pastry Dough (page 64), water and
    short doughs wrapped and chilled
    separately
2 teaspoons peanut or vegetable oil
¼ cup finely chopped onion
1 tablespoon sugar
½ teaspoon soy sauce
1 teaspoon oyster sauce
1 tablespoon hoisin sauce
½ teaspoon toasted sesame oil
1 teaspoon cornstarch dissolved in
    1 tablespoon water
4 ounces Char Siu (page 114), finely diced
1 large egg yolk beaten with 1 teaspoon
    water
1 tablespoon sesame seeds

Unwrap the water dough and place it on a floured board, with one long edge toward you. Unwrap the short dough and center it on top of the water dough, with one short edge toward you. Fold the sides of the water dough over the short dough, with the edges overlapping slightly. Press the overlapping edges and both ends to seal in the short dough completely. Roll out in the direction of the folds to make a rectangle about 6 × 18 inches. Fold the dough in thirds to form a 6-inch square. Cover the dough with plastic wrap and refrigerate for 30 minutes.

Unwrap the dough and roll it out again in the same direction to make a 6 × 18-inch rectangle as before. Fold, wrap, and refrigerate the dough for 30 minutes. Repeat the rolling and folding processes one more time. Cover the dough with plastic wrap and refrigerate it at least 30 minutes, and up to 1 day ahead, before the final rolling and shaping.

Heat a skillet over medium heat; then add the oil. When it is almost smoking, add the onion and stir-fry for 3 minutes, or until transparent. In a small bowl, combine 2 tablespoons water, the sugar, soy

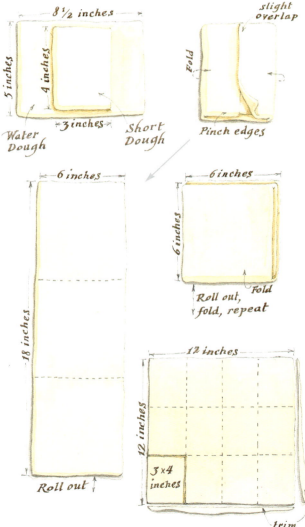

sauce, oyster sauce, hoisin sauce, and sesame oil. Stir into the onion and heat for 30 seconds, or until bubbly. Add the cornstarch mixture and cook for 30 seconds longer, or until the sauce has thickened. Add the char siu and remove from the heat. Transfer the filling to a large plate and divide it into 12 portions. Cool to room temperature.

Roll out the prepared dough into a 13-inch square. Trim off the uneven edges to make a 12-inch square; then cut the dough in thirds crosswise and quarters lengthwise to make twelve 3 × 4-inch rectangles.

Preheat the oven to 400°F.

Place one portion of the filling across the center in the 3-inch direction. Overlap the dough over the filling. Gently press the ends closed. Turn over and place on an ungreased baking sheet. Repeat with the remaining dough and filling, spacing the pastries 1 inch apart on the baking sheet. (At this point, the unbaked pastries may be covered and frozen until firm and then transferred to a plastic bag. Place frozen pastries on a baking sheet as above and let them thaw 30 minutes before proceeding.)

Brush the pastries with the egg yolk mixture; then sprinkle them with sesame seeds. Bake for 25 to 30 minutes, or until golden. Cool briefly on a wire rack and serve warm.

SAVORY TURNOVERS

I used to think these flaky curried meat turnovers would be too difficult to make at home because we always bought them when I was growing up. Once you learn how to make the dough, though, they are not nearly the trouble I imagined. Also, unbaked turnovers freeze well so that last-minute baking is a snap. These are usually filled with curried meat, but many dumpling fillings can be substituted. (Illustrated on page 52.)

MAKES 12 TURNOVERS

2 tablespoons peanut or vegetable oil
4 ounces pork shoulder or boneless,
    skinless chicken (mixture of light and
    dark meat), coarsely ground
½ cup finely chopped onion (1 medium)
1 scallion (white and green parts), finely
    sliced
¼ cup potato, cut in ¼-inch dice
1 celery stalk, finely diced
2 teaspoons curry powder
½ teaspoon salt
¼ teaspoon sugar
1 teaspoon cornstarch mixed with
    2 tablespoons water
Flaky Pastry Dough (page 64), water and
    short doughs wrapped and chilled
    separately
1 large egg yolk beaten with 1 teaspoon
    water

Heat a wok or skillet; then add 1 table-spoon oil. When it is almost smoking, add the pork and stir-fry for 3 to 4 minutes, breaking up the pork with a spatula, until browned. Pour off the fat, and then transfer the pork to a bowl. Add the remaining tablespoon of oil to the wok. When it is very hot, add the onion, scallion, potato, and celery, and stir-fry for 4 to 5 minutes, or until the onion becomes translucent and the potatoes are almost cooked through. Add the pork, curry powder, salt, and sugar, and mix well. Stir in the cornstarch mixture and cook for 30 seconds to 1 minute longer, or until the sauce has thickened. Transfer the filling to a plate and let it cool.

Unwrap both doughs, and cut each dough into 12 portions. Pat out one piece of water dough slightly; then place one piece of short dough onto the center of it. Wrap the water dough around the short dough, pinch-ing the edges of the water dough to enclose the short dough completely. Roll it out to a 3 × 4-inch rectangle.

Starting from a short edge, roll the dough into a cylinder. Turn it so the spiral

Enclose short dough

3 inches

4 inches

Roll out into a
rectangle

Fold in fourths

Roll up

1¾ inch

6 inches

Turn and roll out

3½ inches

Roll out into a circle

Fold in half, and make
a rope border

end is facing you, and then roll it out to a 1¾ × 6-inch rectangle. Beginning with a short edge, fold the dough into fourths. Roll it out to a 3½-inch circle.

Preheat the oven to 400°F.

Spoon 1 tablespoon of the filling onto the center of the circle of dough, leaving enough margin to pinch closed. Fold the dough into a semicircle and pinch the edges together tightly. To make a rope border, place one corner of the dough between your thumb and knuckle of your index finger (see page 31). Pinch; then slide your thumb slightly under the newly pinched edge and roll it up toward the center at the same time you make your next pinch slightly above the first. Continue all around the semicircle.

Place the finished pastries 1 inch apart on an ungreased baking sheet. (At this point, the unbaked pastries may be covered and frozen until firm and then transferred to a plastic bag. Place frozen pastries on a baking sheet as above and let them thaw 30 minutes before proceeding.) Brush the tops with the egg mixture. Bake for 25 to 30 minutes, or until golden brown. (Frozen pastries may require a few more minutes.) Transfer the pastries to a wire rack to cool. Serve hot or at room temperature.

VARIATION
CURRIED VEGETARIAN TURNOVERS

Omit the pork or chicken. Substitute ½ cup finely shredded napa cabbage and increase the diced potato to ⅓ cup. Stir-fry as above, cooking the cabbage with the other vegetables and seasonings.

NAPA CABBAGE

RICE
AND
RICE FLOUR
DISHES

Rice Flour Roll with BEEF

Although dumplings dominate dim sum menus, rice can certainly claim its fair share of dishes, too. Marinated chicken and Chinese sausage top bowls of long-grain rice, infusing the rice with their rich juices. Glutinous rice studded with colorful, savory tidbits shines through inverted glass bowls. Aromatic lotus leaves wrap layers of rice, seasoned meats, and seafood.

Rice flour is also a basis for some popular dishes. I had been making rice flour sheets in an 8-inch square pan that I floated on boiling water in an electric skillet, when I glanced into a restaurant kitchen and saw how they made these on a grand scale. In a corner of a vast wall of steamers were two huge rectangular pans, built in over a vat of boiling water. The sheets that emerged would be cut up not only for rolls, but also into wide noodles to stir-fry as chow fun.

CHICKEN AND SAUSAGE RICE BOWL

At a dim sum restaurant, I once saw an aged, lone diner linger forever over his tea, a newspaper, and just this one dish—an inexpensive, homestyle meal in itself. Some restaurants are very generous with their portions of rice, too; I've had it served in a mixing bowl.

MAKES FOUR 10-OUNCE BOWLS (8 SERVINGS AS PART OF A DIM SUM MEAL)

1⅓ cups long-grain rice, washed and
    drained
1 pound skinless, boneless chicken
    (mixture of light and dark meat), cut in
    ½-inch dice
1 teaspoon soy sauce
1 tablespoon oyster sauce
1 teaspoon salt
1 teaspoon rice wine or dry sherry
2 teaspoons crushed or finely minced
    peeled fresh ginger
1 teaspoon toasted sesame oil
⅛ teaspoon ground white pepper
1 teaspoon cornstarch
2 Chinese sausages, cut in half crosswise
    (optional)
1 scallion (white and green parts), thinly
    sliced

Put the rice in a heavy saucepan with 1⅔ cups water. Cover, bring to a boil, reduce the heat to low, and simmer for 12 to 15 minutes, or until all the water has been absorbed. Remove from the heat and let the rice rest for 5 minutes; then fluff it with a fork. Set aside.

Meanwhile, marinate the chicken with the soy sauce, oyster sauce, salt, rice wine, ginger, sesame oil, white pepper, and cornstarch.

Divide the rice among four 10-ounce bowls, smoothing the top of the rice flat and leaving room for the chicken. Top each portion with one fourth of the chicken, covering the surface of the rice. Place a piece of sausage on top of each portion; then sprinkle with the sliced scallion.

Set up a steamer and bring the water to a boil. Place the bowls in the steamer, cover the pot, and steam over high heat for 12 to 15 minutes, or until the chicken has cooked through. Serve hot.

RICE IN LOTUS LEAF PACKETS

Dried lotus leaves, or water lily pads, make generous, flexible wrappers for this steamed rice dish. The packets unfold to reveal rice, subtly scented by the leaves, studded with chicken, shrimp, pork, mushrooms, and Chinese sausage; they are so filling they are usually shared at the table. As dramatic as the packets appear, they are not difficult to make, and the recipe is easy to adapt for vegetarians. Leftover packets may be frozen.

A package of veined, circular lotus leaves resembles a stack of fans, since they are folded in half before they are dried. Lotus leaves are inexpensive, and they can be stored indefinitely.

MAKES 8 PACKETS

2 cups glutinous rice (sweet rice)
1 teaspoon salt
4 dried shiitake mushrooms
4 dried lotus leaves
2 teaspoons soy sauce
2 teaspoons oyster sauce
1 teaspoon rice wine or dry sherry
¼ teaspoon sugar
2 teaspoons peanut or vegetable oil
4 ounces boneless, skinless chicken
  (mixture of light and dark meat),
  coarsely ground (see Note)
4 ounces shrimp, peeled, deveined, and cut
  in ½-inch chunks (see Note)
1 Chinese sausage, cut in ¼-inch rounds
  (see Note)

2 ounces Char Siu (page 114), cut in
  ¼-inch dice (see Note)
1 tablespoon cornstarch dissolved in
  ½ cup water or chicken broth

Place the rice in a medium bowl with water to cover. Stir the rice gently with a wire whisk to wash it; then pour off the water. Add ½ teaspoon of the salt and enough fresh water to cover the rice by ½ inch, and soak for 2 hours.

Put the shiitake mushrooms in a small bowl and cover them with hot water. Let them stand for 30 to 45 minutes to soften. Drain the mushrooms and cut off and discard the hard stems. Rinse the caps, squeeze them dry, and dice them fine.

Cut each folded lotus leaf in half, into 2 double-layer quarter-circles. Soak them

for 30 minutes in hot water to cover, pressing the leaves down into the water and turning them over occasionally so they are soaked thoroughly.

Rinse the leaves; then shake off the water. Cut about 2 inches off the point, and trim the outer, ragged, curved edge even with scissors. Stack the leaves in the same direction and set aside.

Set up a steamer and bring the water to a boil. Drain the rice thoroughly; then put it in an oiled 2-quart bowl with 1 cup water and the remaining ½ teaspoon salt. Cover and steam the rice for 25 minutes over high heat. Remove it from the heat and allow it to cool slightly in the bowl.

In a small bowl, combine the soy sauce, oyster sauce, rice wine, and sugar. Set aside.

Heat a wok or skillet, and then add the oil. When it is almost smoking, add the chicken and stir-fry for 2 minutes; then add the shrimp and stir-fry for 1 minute longer. Add the mushrooms, Chinese sausage, char siu, and soy sauce mixture, and stir-fry for 1 minute. Stir in the cornstarch mixture and cook for about 1 minute longer, or until the sauce has thickened. Remove from the heat.

Place the stack of leaves with the outer, curved edge facing away from you. Pour a little oil on the top leaf and use your fingertips to spread it evenly over the leaf.

Divide the rice into 8 portions. With wet fingertips, divide one portion of rice in half. Shape each half into a 2 × 3-inch rectangle. Place one rectangle onto the center of the leaf, place about ¼ cup of the meat mixture on top of the rice; then place the other rectangle of rice on top of the meat mixture. Press the layers together gently.

Fold the inner cut end of the leaf up over the rice. Fold in the left and right sides, and then roll the leaf away from you toward the curved edge to make a rectangular packet. Place seam side down on a steamer tier or in a heat-proof dish. Repeat the procedure with the remaining ingredients, to make 8 packets altogether. (At this point, you may cover and refrigerate the packets for up to 24 hours, or place the packets in a plastic bag and freeze them for up to 2 weeks. Thaw completely before steaming.)

Set up a steamer and bring the water to a boil. Steam the packets over high heat for 15 minutes, or until heated through. (Refrigerated packets will require 20 to 25 minutes.) Transfer the packets to a serving plate. To serve, unwrap one packet at a time and place a serving spoon in the rice. Serve hot.

1 Cut in half

2 Cut off point

3 Trim ragged edge

Press together

Fold

Fold sides in

Roll up

NOTE: You can vary the proportions of chicken, shrimp, Chinese sausage, and char siu as long as the total weight is 12 ounces. You can also include or substitute cubed ham, Chinese roast duck, or roast chicken in the mixture.

VARIATION
VEGETARIAN RICE IN LOTUS LEAVES

Substitute vegetarian stir-fry sauce for the oyster sauce. Replace the chicken, shrimp, Chinese sausage, and char siu with 2 cups total of a mixture of cooked, peeled chestnuts, dry-roasted peanuts, finely diced carrots, peeled taro root cut in ½-inch dice, and finely sliced scallions, and stir-fry as above for 4 to 5 minutes, or until the carrots and taro root are barely soft.

GLUTINOUS RICE BOWL

If you have clear glass bowls, you can serve this as many restaurants do, with the bowl inverted over the rice to showcase the ingredients and keep them hot until you are ready to eat. You may easily vary the selection of ingredients in this, as long as you keep the total quantity about the same. A vegetarian variation follows if you want to omit meat altogether.

MAKES FOUR 10-OUNCE BOWLS (8 SERVINGS AS PART OF A DIM SUM MEAL)

2 cups glutinous rice (sweet rice)
1 teaspoon salt
4 dried shiitake mushrooms
8 ounces skinless, boneless chicken (mixture of light and dark meat), cut in ½-inch dice
2 tablespoons soy sauce
1 teaspoon toasted sesame oil
⅛ teaspoon ground white pepper
1 tablespoon peanut or vegetable oil
4 ounces Char Siu (page 114), cut in ½-inch dice (optional)
2 Chinese sausages, cut in ¼-inch rounds
2 scallions (white and green parts), thinly sliced
¼ cup dry-roasted peanuts (optional)
2 tablespoons finely chopped fresh cilantro (optional)
¼ cup peas, fresh or defrosted

In a large bowl, wash and drain the rice. Add ½ teaspoon of the salt and enough water to cover the rice by ½ inch. Soak for 2 hours.

Put the shiitake mushrooms in a small bowl and cover them with hot water. Let them stand for 30 to 45 minutes to soften. Drain the mushrooms and cut off and discard the hard stems. Rinse the caps, squeeze them dry, and dice them fine.

Set up a steamer and bring the water to a boil. Drain the rice thoroughly; then put it in an oiled 2-quart bowl with 1 cup water and the remaining ½ teaspoon of salt. Steam the rice for 25 minutes over high heat. Remove the rice from the heat and allow it to cool slightly in the bowl.

Meanwhile, combine the chicken with 1 tablespoon of the soy sauce, the sesame oil, and white pepper, and marinate for 20 minutes. Heat a wok or skillet; then add 1 tablespoon oil. When it is almost smoking, stir-fry the chicken for 2 minutes over medium-high heat, or until it is barely cooked through. Add the mushrooms, char siu, Chinese sausages, scallions, peanuts, cilantro, and peas and cook for 30 seconds longer. Remove from the heat and gently mix in the rice and the remaining tablespoon of soy sauce until the ingredients are evenly distributed.

GLUTINOUS RICE BOWL

VARIATION

VEGETARIAN GLUTINOUS RICE BOWL

Replace the chicken, char siu, and sausages with 1¾ cups total of a mixture of finely diced carrots, water chestnuts, and taro root, cut in ½-inch dice. Heat a wok or skillet, and then add 1 tablespoon oil. When it is almost smoking, stir-fry the mushrooms, carrots, water chestnuts, and taro root for 3 minutes over medium heat. Then add the scallions, peanuts, cilantro, and peas and stir-fry for 2 to 3 minutes longer, or until the taro root is barely tender. Add the soy sauce, sesame oil, and white pepper, and then gently mix in the rice until the ingredients are evenly distributed. Proceed as above.

Oil four 10-ounce bowls and divide the rice mixture evenly among them, packing it gently and smoothing it even with the tops of the bowls. (At this point, the rice may be covered and refrigerated for 24 hours. Uncover them before steaming.) Set up a steamer, and bring the water to a boil. Place the bowls in the steamer, cover the pot, and steam over high heat for 10 minutes (or 15 minutes if the rice has been refrigerated), or until heated through. Invert each bowl over a separate plate, and unmold the rice just before serving.

TARO ROOT ~ Large variety over 12 inches long

RICE FLOUR SHEETS

Many Chinese grocery stores sell fresh rice flour sheets, but they're not hard to make, and homemade sheets are more tender.

Because the sheets must be steamed in a pan that floats on top of boiling water, you will need a skillet (a square electric skillet is ideal) or roasting pan with a tight-fitting domed lid, that can accommodate an 8- or 9-inch square pan and still allow room for steam to circulate. Using a nonstick pan will make a big difference in how easily the sheet rolls up.

MAKES THREE 8- OR 9-INCH SQUARE SHEETS

¾ cup rice flour (*not* glutinous)
1 tablespoon tapioca starch
¼ teaspoon salt
¼ teaspoon borax powder (optional; see Note)
1 tablespoon peanut or vegetable oil
½ cup boiling water

Oil a nonstick 8- or 9-inch square baking pan. Pour water ¾ inch deep into an electric skillet or roasting pan with a tight-fitting lid, large enough to accommodate the baking pan and allow steam to circulate.

Make a cold water bath by filling a second large pan or a clean sink with 1 inch of cold water.

In a medium bowl, combine the rice flour, tapioca starch, salt, borax powder, if using, and peanut oil. Add ¾ cup water and stir until smooth. Stir in the boiling water.

Bring the water in the skillet or roasting pan to a boil; then reduce the heat so it is barely bubbling. Float the oiled pan on the water to heat it through. Give the batter a quick stir, and ladle ½ cup of the batter into the pan, tilting the pan to spread the batter evenly. Cover and steam for 3 to 4 minutes, or until the sheet has cooked through. Transfer the pan to the cold water bath for 2 minutes.

Use a wide, flat spatula to loosen the sheet along one edge; then roll it up loosely. Transfer the roll to a plate. Repeat with the remaining batter, cleaning and oiling the pan each time, and replenishing the simmering water in the skillet as necessary.

NOTE: Borax powder is also called *pingsha* or boric acid and is sold in small quantities from Chinese herbalists and Asian markets. This may be omitted, but it makes the sheets glossier, more elastic, and less sticky.

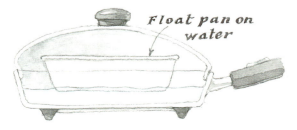

Float pan on water

RICE FLOUR ROLLS WITH BEEF

When you see a trolley stacked with oval dishes covered with stainless steel lids, it's likely to contain different kinds of tender rice flour rolls. In this version, the beef is steamed on top of the batter and then rolled up inside it. The lightly sweetened soy sauce is poured over the rolls just before serving. (Illustrated on page 71.)

MAKES THREE 8- OR 9-INCH ROLLS, EACH CUT IN 5 OR 6 PIECES

8 ounces beef, minced or coarsely ground
1 scallion (white and green parts), thinly
    sliced
¼ teaspoon dried tangerine peel, soaked
    and minced, or fresh tangerine peel,
    finely grated (optional)
¼ teaspoon baking soda
1 teaspoon soy sauce
½ teaspoon sugar
⅛ teaspoon ground white pepper
2 teaspoons toasted sesame oil
1 tablespoon cornstarch
Rice flour sheet batter (see page 78)
Sweet Soy Sauce (page 136)

In a medium bowl, combine the beef, scallion (reserve 2 teaspoons), tangerine peel, baking soda, soy sauce, sugar, white pepper, sesame oil, cornstarch, and ¼ cup water. Squeeze the mixture through your fingers to blend it well; then set aside to marinate for 30 minutes. Divide the mixture into 3 portions, and shape each portion into a loose 8-inch cylinder.

Proceed with cooking and rolling as for rice flour sheets (see page 78), except uncover the pan after cooking the batter the first 30 seconds, and place one portion of the beef down the length of the batter 2 inches from one edge before continuing; when rolling up, begin from the edge closest to the beef.

Cut each roll crosswise into 5 or 6 pieces. Pour the sweet soy sauce over the rolls and sprinkle with the reserved scallions just before serving.

VARIATION
SHRIMP ROLLS

Proceed as for rice flour sheets (see page 78), except place 6 or 7 peeled, cooked medium shrimp in a row along one side of each cooked sheet before rolling. Cut, add sweet soy sauce, and garnish as above.

RICE FLOUR ROLLS
WITH CHINESE SAUSAGE

You'll see trays of these fresh rolls on the counters at many Chinese markets. They are popular for breakfast and snacks as well as dim sum. The batter itself is embedded with numerous savory ingredients before it is steamed, so it needs no additional filling or dipping sauce.

MAKES THREE 8- OR 9-INCH ROLLS, EACH CUT IN 5 OR 6 PIECES

2 teaspoons dried shrimp
1 Chinese sausage, finely diced
1 scallion (white and green parts), thinly
    sliced
¼ cup coarsely chopped fresh cilantro
1 tablespoon sesame seeds, toasted in a
    dry skillet and cooled
Rice flour sheet batter (see page 78)

Put the dried shrimp in a small bowl and cover them with hot water. Let them stand for 30 to 45 minutes to soften; then drain and mince them.

In a medium bowl, mix together the shrimp, Chinese sausage, scallion, cilantro, and sesame seeds; then divide the mixture into 3 portions.

Proceed with cooking and rolling as for rice flour sheets (see page 78), except immediately after tilting the pan to spread the batter, sprinkle one portion of the sausage mixture evenly and quickly over it before it sets, and then cover and proceed. Roll each cooked sheet tightly; then cut each roll into 5 or 6 pieces. Serve warm or at room temperature.

RICE FLOUR ROLLS WITH BEAN SPROUTS

Slivers of char siu, cooked chicken, or roast pork may be used instead of the egg.

MAKES THREE 8- OR 9-INCH ROLLS, EACH CUT IN 5 OR 6 PIECES

Salt

6 ounces bean sprouts (about 3 cups), rinsed and drained, husks and small bits discarded

4 teaspoons peanut or vegetable oil

1 large egg, lightly beaten

2 scallions (white and green parts), cut in 2-inch lengths and shredded

1 cup coarsely grated carrot

1 teaspoon soy sauce

1 teaspoon toasted sesame oil

3 Rice Flour Sheets (page 78)

Soy Vinegar Dip (page 136)

In a large saucepan, bring 4 cups of water to a boil with 1 teaspoon salt. Blanch the bean sprouts over medium-high heat for 30 seconds, or until crisp-tender. Drain the bean sprouts, rinse them under cold water to stop the cooking, and drain again.

Heat a nonstick skillet over medium heat; then add 2 teaspoons of the peanut oil. When it is almost smoking, add the beaten egg, tilting the skillet so the egg covers the bottom evenly. Sprinkle the egg lightly with salt. Reduce the heat to medium-low, and cook the egg for about 1 minute, or until it is just set but not browned. Turn the egg to cook the other side for 10 seconds. Transfer the egg to a plate, let it cool for 5 minutes, and then cut it into fine shreds.

Heat a nonstick skillet over medium heat; then add the remaining 2 teaspoons of the peanut oil. When it is almost smoking, add the scallions and carrot and stir-fry for 30 seconds.

In a large bowl, toss the bean sprouts, egg, scallions, carrot, soy sauce, and sesame oil until well mixed. Divide the mixture into 3 portions. Unroll one rice flour sheet; then spread a portion of the bean sprout mixture along one edge. Starting from the same edge, roll the sheet tightly to enclose the filling. Repeat with the remaining rice flour sheets and filling, making 3 rolls total. Cut each roll crosswise into 5 or 6 pieces. Serve with soy vinegar dip.

GREENS
AND
PAN-FRIED
DISHES

PRODUCE MARKET
in HONG KONG in November

Not everything on the dim sum table comes in a wrapper, dough or otherwise. Stir-fried, griddled, and other dishes offer a good counterpoint to dumplings, and I've often impatiently special-ordered a dish of greens when I haven't seen it come around soon enough on a cart.

One can't help but crave the fresh flavor and texture of greens to balance an overabundance of meat and seafood dishes. You'll often find *gai lan,* Chinese broccoli, which has a pleasantly bitter edge, but if you're lucky, you may also be served pencil-thin asparagus in season or piles of tender young pea shoots.

The Chinese word *heung* translates roughly as "fragrant," and it describes everything from flowers to food. (Hong Kong or *heung keung,* phonetically, for example, means "fragrant harbor," named for the incense that used to be made there.) *Heung* certainly describes a quality of pan-fried foods. Most pan-frying is done in restaurant kitchens, but for a few dishes, a griddle-topped trolley is kept hot so that a waitress can cook your selection right beside your table as other carts swirl around her. Turnip cake, for example, mild-flavored when simply steamed, develops a dark, fragrant crust around its potato-like interior, becoming a different dish altogether with added richness and dimension.

ASPARAGUS

SUGAR SNAP

PEAS

CHINESE BROCCOLI

BROCCOLI RABE

BABY BOK CHOY

BROCCOLINI

CHOY SUM

BROCCOLI

HONG KONG PRODUCE

Walking off a rich dim sum lunch during our visit to Hong Kong, my husband and I wandered into a narrow alleyway just blocks away from the Central District's high-rise office towers. The alley spilled over with bountiful produce stalls, their offerings painstakingly arranged to keep passersby from wandering off to compare the neighbor's prices. As far as we could see, boxes were piled high with thick carrots, daikon radishes the size of my forearm, taro root, sweet potatoes, hard squashes, garlic, cabbages, bittermelons, onions, eggplants, cauliflower, and tomatoes.

Newspapers lined the sidewalk under shallow trays of bright, incendiary peppers. Rustic baskets overflowed next to patched Styrofoam coolers. Cardboard box flaps provided material for crayoned signs haphazardly jammed around every item.

The tenderest Chinese broccoli was carefully trimmed and laid out in neat rows next to a tangle of long beans, a pyramid of baby bok choy, fragrant cilantro, Chinese celery with its roots still attached, fat bunches of flowering chives, asparagus, speckled melons, and myriad unfamiliar greens, all shielded from the sun by makeshift canopies.

The egg vendor scraped eye-catching stripes from the mud coating on thousand-year-old eggs, while the tofu man scooped out hot, soft tofu from a steaming wooden bucket—fast food for a line of impatient office workers.

We rounded a corner to glimpse a butcher gutting a carcass, veered down another side street into a forest of garish, cheap wares and plastic-wrapped blouses, and finally, past a sidewalk eatery. There, oblivious to the passing crowds, whole families or office mates in shirtsleeves balanced themselves on folding chairs set around oilcloth-covered tables and devoured an array of some of the best-looking home-style food I'd seen in a long time.

GREENS WITH OYSTER SAUCE AND OIL

CHOY SUM

Use whatever mild-flavored greens are in season or look most enticing at the market; this dressing complements them all. Because the dish is served cold or at room temperature, it may be cooked several hours ahead and dressed at the last minute.

MAKES 4 TO 6 SERVINGS AS PART OF A DIM SUM MENU

1 pound greens, such as *gai lan* (Chinese broccoli), *choy sum*, broccoli, broccolini, broccoli rabe, asparagus, baby bok choy, or sugar snap peas
1 teaspoon salt
1 teaspoon soy sauce
1 tablespoon oyster sauce
1 teaspoon peanut or vegetable oil
2 teaspoons toasted sesame oil
1 teaspoon cornstarch dissolved in 2 tablespoons water

Trim the tough ends off the greens. (You may also want to pare the lower portions.) Leave small baby bok choy intact; trim to separate larger leaves. Remove the strings from the sugar snap peas.

In a large saucepan, bring 6 cups of water and the salt to a boil. Add the greens and blanch them for 4 to 7 minutes, or until they are crisp-tender. (Sugar snap peas require only 1 minute.) Drain in a colander and rinse gently under cold water to stop the cooking. Shake off the water or pat the greens dry. Cut long pieces to about 3 inches. The greens may be made early in the day up to this point, covered, and refrigerated.

In a small saucepan, mix the soy sauce, oyster sauce, peanut oil, and sesame oil until well blended. Heat the mixture over medium heat for about 1 minute, until bubbly, and then stir in the cornstarch mixture and cook for about 30 seconds longer, or until the sauce has thickened. Let the sauce cool slightly. Arrange the greens on a serving plate; then drizzle the sauce over them. If you prefer, you can toss the greens with the sauce first, and then arrange them on a serving plate. Serve at room temperature or cold.

PEA SHOOTS WITH GARLIC

Small bits of garlic fleck the mild, bright-green pea shoots in this simple dish. A bagful of pea shoots in Chinatown is remarkably inexpensive—look for tender ones, with as few tough, curled tendrils as possible, as these need to be pinched off before they are cooked.

MAKES 4 TO 6 SERVINGS AS PART OF A
DIM SUM MEAL

8 ounces pea shoots
½ teaspoon salt, plus additional to taste
1 tablespoon peanut or vegetable oil
2 or 3 garlic cloves, finely diced
1 teaspoon toasted sesame oil
1 teaspoon soy sauce

Rinse and drain the pea shoots. Pinch off and discard any large, tough stems or long, curled tendrils. In a large saucepan, bring 2 quarts of water and ½ teaspoon salt to a boil. Add the pea shoots and blanch them for 2 minutes. Taste a pea shoot; it should have a pleasant crunch, but not be overly chewy. Drain the pea shoots in a colander, rinse them under cold water to stop the cooking, and drain them well.

Heat a skillet over medium heat; then heat the peanut oil. When it is almost smoking, add the garlic, reduce the heat to low, and stir-fry for 2 minutes, or until the garlic becomes translucent. Do not let the garlic brown or it will become bitter. Remove from the heat, add the sesame oil, soy sauce, pea shoots, and salt to taste, and toss to mix well. Transfer to a serving plate. Serve at room temperature.

VARIATION

Blanch 12 ounces pea shoots, squeeze them dry, and then chop them. Proceed as above, using 4 garlic cloves and 1½ teaspoons each toasted sesame oil and soy sauce. Proceed as directed for Scallop Dumplings (page 26), substituting the pea shoot mixture for the scallop filling. You can also add 3 tablespoons minced water chestnuts, or ¼ cup finely diced char siu, cooked chicken, or shrimp. Pea shoot dumplings do not freeze well.

STUFFED MUSHROOMS

If the quantity of mushrooms in this recipe seems too large, you'll be surprised how quickly they disappear hot from the skillet.

MAKES 24 STUFFED MUSHROOMS

24 mushrooms, 1¾ to 2 inches in diameter, such as fresh or dried shiitake, or fresh brown or white

3 to 4 water chestnuts, peeled and finely diced

1 scallion (white and green parts), finely minced

8 ounces pork shoulder, coarsely ground

4 ounces shrimp, peeled, deveined, and coarsely chopped

2 teaspoons soy sauce

½ teaspoon salt

¼ teaspoon sugar

2 teaspoons rice wine or dry sherry

2 tablespoons peanut or vegetable oil

If using dried shiitake mushrooms, put them in a large saucepan and cover them with hot water. Cover, bring to a boil, then turn off the heat. Keep the saucepan covered, and let the mushrooms stand for 30 to 45 minutes to soften. Drain the mushrooms and cut off and discard the hard stems. Rinse the caps, squeeze them to remove the water, then pat them as dry as possible with a towel.

Wipe fresh mushrooms clean with a damp towel. Remove the stems.

Preheat the oven to 200°F.

In a medium bowl, combine the water chestnuts, scallion, pork, shrimp, soy sauce, salt, sugar, and rice wine. Squeeze the filling through your fingers to blend it well.

Press a rounded teaspoon of the filling firmly into each mushroom cap, smoothing out the edges with wet fingertips.

Heat a large, nonstick skillet, then add 1 tablespoon of the oil. When it is almost smoking, add half of the mushrooms, filling side down. Press down gently to flatten the filling slightly, and cook over medium heat for 2 to 3 minutes, or until well browned. Turn over and cook for 2 minutes on the other side; then add ⅓ cup water and reduce the heat to low. Continue to cook, uncovered, for 10 to 12 minutes, or until the mushrooms are tender and all the liquid has evaporated.

Transfer the mushrooms to a serving plate and keep them warm in the oven. Clean the skillet, heat the remaining tablespoon of oil, and cook the remaining mushrooms. Serve hot.

STUFFED BELL PEPPERS

After an endless parade of dumplings, crunchy bell peppers provide a welcome change for both the eyes and the palate. Make some of these with yellow or red bell peppers for even more color. The filling is also used to stuff triangles of firm tofu.

MAKES 24 PIECES

FILLING

10 ounces shrimp, peeled, deveined, and coarsely ground or chopped
1 scallion (white and green parts), finely minced
1 teaspoon salt
2 teaspoons rice wine or dry sherry
⅛ teaspoon ground white pepper
1 teaspoon cornstarch

2 or 3 bell peppers, cut into twenty-four 2 × 1½-inch rectangles
Peanut or vegetable oil, for pan-frying

SAUCE

⅓ cup Chicken Stock (page 39) or canned, low-sodium chicken broth
1 teaspoon soy sauce
2 teaspoons oyster sauce
¼ teaspoon sugar
8 fermented black beans, rinsed and drained (optional)
1½ teaspoons cornstarch dissolved in 1 tablespoon water

Preheat the oven to 200°F.

TO MAKE THE FILLING In a medium bowl, combine the shrimp, scallion, salt, rice wine, pepper, and cornstarch. Squeeze the filling through your fingers to blend it well.

Press a heaping teaspoon of the filling into each piece of bell pepper, smoothing the filling to the edges of the pepper.

Heat a large, nonstick skillet over medium heat; then add 1 tablespoon of oil. When it is almost smoking, add one layer of stuffed peppers, filling side down. Use a spatula to press down lightly on each piece to flatten out the filling. Cook for 2 to 3 minutes, until well browned. Turn, add 2 tablespoons water, and cook uncovered for 4 to 5 minutes, or until the water has evaporated and the peppers are crisp-tender. Transfer the

Stuffed Bell Peppers

peppers, filling side up, to a serving plate, and keep them warm in the oven while you cook the remaining peppers.

TO MAKE THE SAUCE In a small saucepan, combine the chicken stock, soy sauce, oyster sauce, and sugar. Mash the fermented black beans slightly between your fingers; then add them to the sauce mixture. Bring the sauce to a boil, and then stir in the cornstarch mixture. Reduce the heat to medium-low, and cook for about 1 minute, or until the sauce has thickened. Drizzle the sauce over the peppers. Serve hot.

VARIATION
STUFFED TOFU

MAKES 16 PIECES

Replace the bell pepper with two 10-ounce blocks of firm tofu. Preheat the oven to 200°F. Make a half-recipe of the filling. Cut each block of tofu in half along a narrow side to form 2 squares, each about 3 × 3 × ¾ inches. Cut each square from corner to corner in an X-shape to form 4 triangles. Repeat with the remaining squares, making 16 triangles in all. Pat the tofu dry with a paper towel.

Place the long side of each triangle facedown; then make 2 angled cuts

halfway down the short sides to cut out a wedge-shaped pocket. Place a scant teaspoon of the filling into each pocket, being careful not to break the tofu.

Heat a nonstick skillet over medium heat; then add 1 tablespoon oil. When it is almost smoking, place several pieces of tofu, one filled side down, into the skillet. Do not crowd. Turn the tofu to brown all sides, starting with the filling sides, and cooking for 5 to 6 minutes total. Transfer the tofu to a serving plate and keep it warm in the oven while you cook the remaining tofu. Make the sauce as above and drizzle it over the tofu. Serve hot.

STUFFED TOFU

TURNIP CAKE

This dish is called turnip cake, but it is neither made with turnips nor is it a cake; its texture is closer to thick mashed potatoes. Its main ingredient, daikon radish, is milder than red radishes, and it mellows further as it cooks. It is sometimes made without embellishment, but I like it studded with bits of Chinese sausage, dried shrimp, and scallions. The cake can be served straight out of the steamer, but it is best when pan-fried until crisp on both sides.

You can steam the cake a day or two ahead, refrigerate it, and then pan-fry it at the last minute, but it does not freeze well.

MAKES ONE 9-INCH ROUND CAKE CUT IN
10 TO 24 PIECES

1 tablespoon small dried shrimp (optional)
12 ounces daikon radish, pared and
    coarsely shredded (about 2½ cups,
    lightly packed)
2 teaspoons peanut or vegetable oil, plus
    additional for pan-frying
1 Chinese sausage, finely diced
1 scallion (white and green parts), finely
    sliced
1 tablespoon finely chopped fresh
    cilantro
1¾ cups rice flour (*not*
    glutinous)
1½ teaspoons salt
½ teaspoon sugar
¼ teaspoon ground white
    pepper

If using the dried shrimp, put them in a small bowl and cover them with hot water. Let them stand for 30 to 45 minutes to soften. Drain; then mince the shrimp.

Put the shredded daikon radish in a saucepan with 1½ cups water. Bring the mixture to a boil, reduce the heat to low, and cook for 15 minutes, or until tender. Remove the mixture from the heat.

Measure the radish with its cooking water (using a 1-quart measuring cup if you have one) and add enough water to make 3 cups. Transfer the mixture to a large bowl and cool to lukewarm.

Heat a large skillet; then add the 2 teaspoons of oil. When it is almost smoking, stir-fry the Chinese sausage, scallion, and dried shrimp for 1 minute. Stir in the cilantro and remove the mixture from the heat. Set it aside.

T U R N I P   C A K E

Mix the rice flour, salt, sugar, and white pepper. Add the mixture to the radish and its cooking water, and stir to make a thick batter. Stir in the Chinese sausage mixture.

Oil a 9-inch round cake pan. Pour the mixture into the pan. Set up a steamer and bring the water to a boil. Steam the turnip cake for 40 minutes over high heat, replenishing the water in the pot as necessary.

Remove the turnip cake from the steamer and allow it to cool to room temperature. (The turnip cake may be covered and refrigerated up to 2 days ahead at this point.) Cut into diamonds or squares. Heat a skillet over medium-high heat; then add 1 tablespoon oil. When it is almost smoking, pan-fry several pieces of turnip cake for about 3 minutes, or until browned. then turn to brown the other side. Add oil to the pan as necessary. Serve hot.

VARIATIONS

✦ For a vegetarian version, omit the Chinese sausage and dried shrimp, and use 2 finely sliced scallions. For additional color, you may also add 3 tablespoons of finely diced carrots. Stir-fry the carrots with the scallions and cilantro.

✦ If not pan-frying, uncover the steamer about a minute before the turnip cake is done, sprinkle the top with 1 tablespoon each of toasted sesame seeds and finely sliced scallions, cover, and finish steaming.

DAIKON RADISH

DEEP-FRIED AND BEAN CURD SHEET DISHES

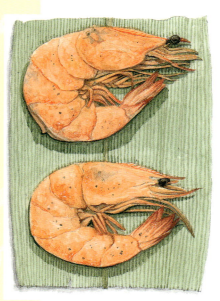

Who can resist the satisfying richness of deep-fried dim sum treats? Creamy taro dumplings develop a delicately crisp crust in hot oil, and pork dumplings turn delightfully chewy. Crab claws, wrapped in a shrimp mixture, are fried until golden. Whole prawns, still sizzling in their shells, are generously sprinkled with a pepper-salt mixture and minced garlic; silky eggplant is stuffed with shrimp; seaweed wraps are filled with nuggets of chopped pork and shrimp; and crunchy spring roll wrappers or bean curd sheets enclose shredded vegetables and meats.

Soybean-based bean curd sheets are also used for vegetarian mock chicken; when the rolled-up sheets are cut crosswise, their mushroom "bones" and soy sauce glaze fools the eye into seeing sliced, roast chicken.

SETTING UP FOR DEEP FRYING

Deep-frying used to seem messy, greasy, and even a bit dangerous. I remember my mother emptying gallon-size cans of oil into her restaurant-size wok with its own gas burner and then heating it until it shimmered. A roar like a cheering crowd would erupt the moment food touched the oil.

I've since discovered it is possible to enjoy deep-fried foods without using vast amounts of oil or special equipment. I use a wok on a sturdy stand, a heavy dutch oven, or even a large, heavy saucepan if I'm only cooking a small quantity. A candy thermometer registers changes in the oil temperature as you add or remove food; raise or reduce the heat as necessary to make sure the food will cook properly. Overheated oil overbrowns foods before they are cooked through; underheated oil makes food heavy and soggy instead of giving it a crisp exterior.

I prefer the flavor of peanut oil for deep-frying, but I've also used vegetable oil. Avoid olive oil. If you are frying several foods, start with the mildest in flavor and use a strainer to remove stray bits of food as you go. I do not reuse oil because its flavor and smoking temperature change after the first go-round.

A few precautions are in order when working with hot oil. Never overfill your cooking vessel; oil should be deep enough to allow food to float as it cooks, but leave at least 2 inches of space at the top so the oil does not boil over and so food has space to expand. Don't turn your back while you are deep-frying. Make sure handles cannot be reached by children, either while you are cooking or while the oil is cooling afterward. Keep a fire extinguisher nearby; a large wok lid or pot lid may also smother a small fire, but never pour water on an oil fire.

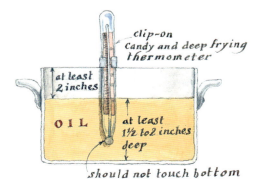

clip-on
Candy and deep frying
thermometer

at least
2 inches

OIL   at least
1½ to 2 inches
deep

should not touch bottom

TARO DUMPLINGS

This richest of dumplings can be leaden in an indifferent cook's hands, but on my last day in Hong Kong, the ones I ordered were ethereal, with a crust that turned into gossamer lace; golden fluffs of it melted in my mouth.

My many efforts to duplicate it were in vain, but then I've never seen their equal anywhere else, either. Still, a hot, fresh homemade taro dumpling is no small treat. The dough forms its own delicately crisp woven-textured crust with an inner creaminess like the fluffiest mashed potatoes around a savory bite of seasoned pork and shrimp. Watch the oil temperature carefully for the lightest crust, and serve immediately if possible.

MAKES 12 DUMPLINGS

FILLING

2 dried shiitake mushrooms
2 teaspoons peanut or vegetable oil
2 ounces pork shoulder, cut in ¼-inch dice
1 ounce shrimp, peeled, deveined, and cut in ¼-inch dice
1 scallion (white and green parts), thinly sliced
½ teaspoon soy sauce
½ teaspoon rice wine or dry sherry
½ teaspoon toasted sesame oil
¼ teaspoon salt
⅛ teaspoon ground white pepper
1 teaspoon cornstarch dissolved in 1 tablespoon cold water

DOUGH

10 ounces taro root, peeled and cut into ½-inch dice
2 tablespoons vegetable shortening
3 tablespoons cornstarch
1 teaspoon sugar
⅛ teaspoon ground white pepper
1 teaspoon baking powder

Peanut or vegetable oil for deep-frying

TO MAKE THE FILLING Put the shiitake mushrooms in a small bowl and cover them with hot water. Let them stand for 30 to 45 minutes to soften. Drain the mushrooms and cut off and discard the hard stems. Rinse the caps, squeeze them dry, and dice fine.

Heat a wok or large skillet over high heat; then add the peanut oil. When it is almost smoking, add the pork, shrimp,

mushrooms, and scallion, and stir-fry for 2 minutes. Add the soy sauce, rice wine, sesame oil, salt, and white pepper and cook for 30 seconds. Stir in the cornstarch mixture and cook for 30 seconds longer, or until thickened. Remove the mixture from the heat and let it cool. Divide the mixture into 12 portions. Cover and refrigerate while preparing the dough.

TO MAKE THE DOUGH Set up a steamer, and then bring the water to a boil. Steam the taro root for 20 to 30 minutes, or until soft. Transfer it to a deep, flat-bottomed dish, add the shortening, and mash it while it is still hot. Let it cool for 5 minutes.

In a small bowl, combine the cornstarch, sugar, white pepper, and baking powder. Add the mixture to the mashed taro root and knead to make a well-blended and smooth dough. Add ¼ cup water and knead the dough again. It should have the consistency of soft mashed potatoes. Add 1 to 2 tablespoons more water if necessary. Divide the dough into 12 lumps.

TO MAKE THE DUMPLINGS Wet your hands and hold one lump of dough in your palm. Flatten the lump slightly; then put 1 portion of the filling onto the center. Mold the dough completely around the filling in a smooth football shape. Repeat with the remaining dough and filling.

Line a baking sheet with several layers of paper towels. Pour 4 to 6 cups of oil in a wok or heavy pot. (The amount of oil you use will depend on the size of your vessel, but the oil should be at least 1½ to 2 inches deep, and no closer than 2 inches to the top.) Clip a candy thermometer to the side of your vessel and heat the oil to 340°F.

One at a time, carefully put 2 or 3 dumplings into the oil. (More will reduce the oil temperature too much.) Rotate the dumplings with a slotted spoon, and cook for 2 to 2½ minutes, or until well browned. Adjust the heat as necessary to keep the oil above 325°F. Remove the dumplings with a slotted spoon or wire strainer and drain them on the baking sheet. Cook the remaining dumplings 2 or 3 at a time, using a fine mesh sieve to scoop out stray bits from the oil between batches. Serve hot or warm.

VARIATION

Replace the filling with 12 medium peeled, cooked shrimp. Enclose 1 shrimp in each portion of dough, rolling the dough into a ball, and proceed as above.

TARO ROOT

Small variety about 3 inches long

DEEP-FRIED PORK DUMPLINGS

I associate these hom suey gok *with the intense flavor of salted, preserved turnip because my grandmother always included it in her filling. Although the glutinous rice flour dough won't brown much, deep-frying gives it a light, crisp exterior that contrasts with a pleasant chewiness within.*

MAKES 12 DUMPLINGS (YOU MAY CUT EACH IN HALF FOR 24 PIECES)

FILLING

4 dried shiitake mushrooms
2 teaspoons dried shrimp (optional)
1 teaspoon soy sauce
1 teaspoon rice wine or dry sherry
¼ teaspoon sugar
4 ounces pork shoulder, cut into ¼-inch dice
2 teaspoons peanut or vegetable oil
1 tablespoon salted, preserved turnip, rinsed, squeezed dry, and finely minced (see Note)
1 scallion (white and green parts), thinly sliced
1 teaspoon cornstarch mixed with 2 teaspoons water

DOUGH

1½ cups glutinous rice flour
2 tablespoons wheat starch, plus additional for dusting the board
¼ cup sugar
¼ teaspoon salt
1 teaspoon peanut or vegetable oil
¾ cup boiling water

Peanut or vegetable oil, for deep-frying

TO MAKE THE FILLING Put the shiitake mushrooms and dried shrimp, if using, in separate small bowls and cover them with hot water. Let them stand for 30 to 45 minutes to soften. Drain the mushrooms and cut off and discard the hard stems. Rinse the caps, squeeze them dry, and mince fine. Drain, and then mince the shrimp.

In a medium bowl, combine the soy sauce, rice wine, and sugar. Add the pork, stirring to mix well. Marinate for 30 minutes.

Heat a wok or skillet; then add the oil. When it is almost smoking, add the pork and stir-fry over medium-high heat for 2 to 3 minutes, until lightly browned. Add the mushrooms, dried shrimp, preserved turnip, and scallion and stir-fry for 1 minute longer. Add the cornstarch mixture and cook for 30 seconds longer, or until the sauce has thickened. Let the filling cool while you make the dough. (The filling may be covered and refrigerated for up to 24 hours.) Divide the filling into 12 portions.

TO MAKE THE DOUGH In a large bowl, whisk together the glutinous rice flour, wheat starch, sugar, and salt. With a wooden spoon, stir in the oil; then stir in the boiling water until well blended. Lightly dust a board with wheat starch. Turn the dough out and knead briefly to incorporate the ingredients. Divide the dough into 12 portions.

TO MAKE THE DUMPLINGS Put a little water in a small bowl. Flatten one piece of dough between your palms into a 3-inch circle. Place one portion of the filling onto the center. Dip a finger in the water and wet the edge halfway around; then fold the circle in half and pinch the edges together firmly to seal. It is important to seal the dumplings well to keep them from bursting open during cooking. Set the finished dumplings on a baking sheet lightly dusted with wheat starch. Repeat with the remaining ingredients.

Pour 4 to 6 cups of oil in a wok or heavy pot. (The amount of oil you use will depend on the size of your vessel, but the oil should be at least 1½ to 2 inches deep,

and no closer than 2 inches to the top.) Clip a candy thermometer to the side of the vessel and heat the oil to 360°F. Line a baking sheet with several layers of paper towels. One at a time, carefully put 2 or 3 dumplings into the oil. Cook for about 5 minutes, turning the dumplings to cook them evenly. The dumplings will barely brown, but they should puff up and develop a bubbly surface. Remove the dumplings with a slotted spoon or wire strainer and drain them on the baking sheet. Cook the remaining dumplings 2 or 3 at a time. If desired, cut the dumplings in half with kitchen scissors and transfer them to a serving plate just before serving. Serve hot.

NOTE: Salted, preserved turnip has a strong flavor. It will mellow when cooked with other ingredients, but you may omit it if you prefer and substitute ½ teaspoon salt.

Salted, Preserved TURNIP

DEEP-FRIED CRAB CLAWS

I don't know anyone who doesn't love these, but I thought I would have to spend a fortune on a pile of crabs just to have enough claws for everyone. Then I discovered some Asian markets carry packages of frozen claws for less than I would have to pay for a single local Dungeness crab.

If you can't find crab claws, don't be discouraged; improvise, because these are too good to pass up. Use a single whole crab, substituting the tips of each leg for the claw shells. If crabs are out of season, use frozen crabmeat, and omit the shells altogether.

MAKES 12 PIECES

12 frozen crab claws or 1 whole crab
   (1½ to 2 pounds)
1 pound shrimp, peeled, deveined, and
   ground or finely chopped
2 scallions (white and green parts), finely
   minced
¼ cup mixture of finely minced celery,
   carrot, and water chestnuts
1 large egg white, lightly beaten
1 teaspoon salt
1 teaspoon rice wine or dry sherry
¼ teaspoon sugar
½ teaspoon toasted sesame oil
1 teaspoon cornstarch
1 cup fine bread crumbs (from about
   3 slices of white bread)
Peanut or vegetable oil, for deep-frying

CHOICE OF DIPPING SAUCES
Sweet and Sour Sauce (page 137)
2 teaspoons hot dry mustard, such as
   Colman's, mixed with 1 tablespoon
   water
Bottled chili sauce

If using frozen crab claws, thaw them; then rinse them and pat them dry.

If using a whole crab, use kitchen scissors to cut off the pointed tip along with a small part of the next joint, from each crab leg. Cut off both claws and separate their nippers, trimming off any sharp edges. You should have 12 trimmed shell pieces in all. Rinse them and pat them dry. Extract the crabmeat, keeping the large pieces of leg meat as intact as possible.

Preheat the oven to 200°F.

Line a baking sheet with several layers of paper towels and set aside.

frozen claw

Cut off leg tips and claws

DEEP-FRIED CRAB CLAWS

In a bowl, combine the shrimp, scallions, diced vegetables, egg white, salt, rice wine, sugar, sesame oil, and cornstarch, squeezing the mixture through your fingers to blend it well. Divide the mixture into 12 portions.

Place the bread crumbs in a pie plate or deep dish. Wet your hands, and then flatten one portion of the shrimp mixture in your palm. Place a thawed crab claw, piece of crab leg meat, or a scant tablespoon of crabmeat on top of the shrimp mixture, and wrap the shrimp mixture around it, forming an oval shape. If using, insert a leg shell in one end and mold the shrimp mixture around it to hold it in place with the shell tip protruding.

Roll the piece in the bread crumbs; then squeeze it lightly to press the crumbs gently into the shrimp mixture. Place the finished pieces on a plate and repeat with the remaining ingredients.

Pour 4 to 6 cups of oil in a wok or heavy pot. (The amount of oil you use will depend on the size of your vessel, but the oil should be at least 1½ to 2 inches deep, and no closer than 2 inches to the top.) Clip a candy thermometer to the side of the vessel and heat the oil to 325°F. With a slotted spoon, carefully lower 4 to 6 pieces, one at a time, into the oil. Turn them several times to brown evenly, and cook for 3 to 4 minutes, or until cooked through. The pieces will not rise to the surface, so check to make sure they are not browning too quickly. Remove the pieces with a slotted spoon and drain them on the baking sheet.

Transfer the cooked pieces to a serving plate and keep them warm in the oven while you cook the remaining pieces. Serve hot with your choice of dipping sauces.

DEEP-FRIED STUFFED EGGPLANT

Like pan-fried stuffed bell peppers, this features a tasty shrimp filling. Here it is wedged into a slice of eggplant before it is fried to silky perfection and glazed with a light sauce punctuated with fermented black beans.

MAKES 14 TO 16 PIECES

FILLING

6 ounces shrimp, peeled, deveined, and coarsely ground or chopped
1 scallion (green part only), minced
½ teaspoon salt
1 teaspoon rice wine or dry sherry
1 teaspoon cornstarch

EGGPLANT

1 large egg
⅓ cup all-purpose flour
3 tablespoons cornstarch
¼ teaspoon salt, plus additional for salting the eggplant
1 pound Chinese or Japanese eggplants (see Note)
Peanut or vegetable oil, for deep-frying

SAUCE

2 teaspoons peanut or vegetable oil
1 scallion (white and green parts), thinly sliced
½ cup Chicken Stock (page 39) or canned, low-sodium chicken broth
1 teaspoon fermented black beans, rinsed and lightly mashed (optional)
½ teaspoon soy sauce
¼ teaspoon salt
¼ teaspoon sugar
1 teaspoon cornstarch dissolved in 1 tablespoon water

TO MAKE THE FILLING In a medium bowl, mix the shrimp, scallion, salt, rice wine, and cornstarch, squeezing the mixture through your fingers to blend it well. Set aside.

TO PREPARE THE EGGPLANT In a medium bowl, beat the egg with 1 tablespoon water and set aside. Sift together the flour, cornstarch, and salt into a deep dish. Line 1 or 2 baking sheets with several layers of paper towels and set aside.

Cut off the ends diagonally from the eggplants and discard them. Cut the eggplants diagonally into 1-inch thick ovals, making 14 to 16 pieces total. Cut out a deep wedge ¼ inch wide, from the side of each piece. It should go about two-thirds

←—1 inch—→

of the way through each slice. Salt the egg-plant pieces and let stand for 20 minutes.

Preheat the oven to 200°F.

Wipe the pieces with paper towels to remove the salt and moisture. Stuff about a teaspoon of the shrimp mixture into the cavity in each piece of eggplant.

Pour about 4 to 6 cups of oil of in a wok or heavy pot. (The amount will vary depending on the size of your vessel, but the oil should be at least 1½ to 2 inches deep and no closer than 2 inches to the top.) Clip a candy thermometer to the side of the vessel and heat the oil to 350°F.

Dip each piece of eggplant in the egg mixture and then in the flour mixture, shaking off any excess flour. Carefully lower 4 pieces into the oil, one at a time, and cook for 4 to 5 minutes, turning sev-eral times to brown evenly. Remove the pieces with a slotted spoon or wire strainer and drain on the baking sheet. Transfer the pieces to a serving plate and keep them warm in the oven while you cook the remaining pieces.

TO MAKE THE SAUCE Heat a skillet over medium heat, and then add the oil. When it is almost smoking, add the scallion and stir-fry for 30 seconds, or until bright green. Add the chicken stock; fermented black beans, if using; soy sauce; salt; and sugar, and bring the sauce to a boil. Stir in the cornstarch mixture and continue cook-ing for 1 minute, or until the sauce has thickened. Put the eggplant pieces on a serving plate, and drizzle the sauce over them, or put the sauce in a small bowl to serve on the side as a dipping sauce. Serve hot.

NOTE: If Chinese or Japanese eggplants are unavailable, see the variation below for using globe eggplants.

VARIATION

To substitute globe eggplants for the Chinese or Japanese eggplants, cut off and discard the ends. Cut the eggplants into ½-inch-thick rounds; then cut into semicircles, for 14 to 16 pieces total. Spread a layer of the shrimp mixture on top of each slice of eggplant, smooth-ing it off evenly around the edges. Proceed as above.

CHINESE or JAPANESE EGGPLANT

SEAWEED-WRAPPED ROLLS

This unusual dim sum is reminiscent of Japanese nori *sushi; the same kind of seaweed wraps the filling. Instead of rice, however, the filling is a ginger-spiked meat and shrimp mixture, and deep-frying crisps the seaweed.*

MAKES 12 ROLLS (OR 24 HALVES)

FILLING

6 ounces pork shoulder or chicken
   (mixture of light and dark meat),
   coarsely ground or chopped
6 ounces shrimp, peeled, deveined, and cut
   in ¼-inch dice
6 finely minced water chestnuts
1 scallion (white and green parts), thinly
   sliced
1 tablespoon finely minced peeled fresh
   ginger
1 teaspoon soy sauce
½ teaspoon salt
¼ teaspoon sugar
⅛ teaspoon ground white pepper
2 teaspoons toasted sesame oil
1 teaspoon cornstarch

SEAWEED WRAPS

3 sheets of *nori* seaweed, each cut in four
   2-inch-wide strips
1 tablespoon all-purpose flour

BATTER

¼ cup all-purpose flour
2 tablespoons cornstarch
¼ teaspoon salt

Peanut or vegetable oil, for deep-frying
Sweet and Sour Sauce (page 137, optional)

TO MAKE THE FILLING   In a bowl, combine the filling ingredients. Squeeze the filling through your fingers to blend it well. With wet hands, divide the filling into 12 portions, and then shape each portion into a 2½-inch-long cylinder.

    Preheat the oven to 200°F.

TO WRAP THE ROLLS Roll a strip of seaweed around each portion of filling. The seaweed should wrap around the filling completely. Flatten the ends of the filling even with the edges of the seaweed. Put the flour on a plate. Dip each end of the seaweed rolls in the flour, shaking off any excess flour.

TO MAKE THE BATTER In a small bowl, combine the flour, cornstarch, salt, and ½ cup water and stir until the batter is smooth.

Pour about 4 to 6 cups of oil in a wok or heavy pot. (The amount of oil you use will depend on the size of your vessel, but the oil should be at least 1½ to 2 inches deep, and no closer than 2 inches to the top.) Clip a candy thermometer to the side of the vessel and heat the oil to 350°F. Line a baking sheet with several layers of paper towels.

One at a time, dip 3 or 4 rolls into the batter, letting the excess drip back into the bowl; then carefully lower them into the oil. Stir the rolls with a slotted spoon to brown them evenly, and fry for 4 minutes, or until cooked through. Remove the rolls with a slotted spoon and drain them on the baking sheet.

Transfer the rolls to a serving plate and keep warm in the oven while you fry the remaining rolls. If desired, cut each roll in half crosswise. Serve hot or at room temperature with sweet and sour sauce, if desired.

WATER CHESTNUTS

SALT-FRIED WHOLE PRAWNS

It's impossible to eat these prawns delicately, but after the first one, you won't care. As a child, I learned to hold prawns with chopsticks while I peeled them with my teeth, but you needn't be so fussy. Serve these piping hot, generously sprinkled with minced garlic and peppersalt and provide your guests with plenty of paper napkins. (Illustrated on page 92.)

MAKES 16 TO 20 PRAWNS

1 pound prawns in shells, preferably with
    heads (size 16 to 20 count)
2 tablespoons cornstarch
Peanut or vegetable oil, for deep-frying
1 garlic clove, finely minced
Peppersalt with Chinese Five-Spice Powder
    (page 135)

Preheat the oven to 200°F.

With a sharp, preferably serrated, knife, carefully cut through the shell along the back of each prawn just deep enough to expose the sand vein. Remove the vein, rinse and drain the prawns; then pat them dry with paper towels. Place 8 to 10 prawns in a paper or plastic bag with 1 tablespoon of the cornstarch. Hold the bag closed and shake it gently to distribute the cornstarch evenly over the prawns.

Line a baking sheet with several layers of paper towels. Pour 4 to 6 cups of oil in a wok or heavy pot. (The amount of oil you use will depend on the size of your vessel, but the oil should be at least 1½ to 2 inches deep, and no closer than 2 inches to the top.) Clip a candy thermometer to the side of the vessel and heat the oil to 325°F. Carefully lower the dredged prawns, one at a time, into the oil. Stir the prawns gently to separate and cook evenly. Cook the prawns for 2 to 3 minutes, or until they are lightly browned. Adjust the heat to maintain a temperature of at least 275°F.

Remove the prawns with a wire strainer or slotted spoon, and drain them briefly on the baking sheet. Pat the prawns gently with additional paper towels. Transfer the prawns to a large bowl, and toss them with the garlic and a generous sprinkling of the peppersalt mixture. Keep warm in the oven.

Use a fine mesh strainer to scoop out stray brown bits from the oil; then reheat the oil to 325°F. Dredge the remaining prawns with the remaining 1 tablespoon cornstarch, fry as above, and toss with the seasoned prawns. Transfer the prawns to a serving plate. Serve hot.

cut along back

SPRING ROLLS

Egg rolls are so widely enjoyed in America, offered in even the most remote (and least authentic) Chinese restaurants, that I suspected that they might be an American invention, like chop suey. In fact these fried bundles are quite traditional, though I did learn they are only called egg rolls in the West, perhaps in reference to the egg in their flour-based wrappers. I also learned they got their other name, spring rolls, because they were originally served to celebrate the arrival of spring. They may be filled with myriad combinations and paired with a wide choice of dipping sauces. With packaged wrappers, this is an easy recipe, but if they are not available, use the recipe on page 23.

MAKES 8 SPRING ROLLS, EACH CUT IN 3 PIECES

FILLING
2 ounces pork shoulder or boneless chicken breast, cut in matchsticks
2 ounces shrimp, peeled, deveined, and cut in ½-inch chunks
2 teaspoons soy sauce
2 teaspoons rice wine or dry sherry

1 teaspoon toasted sesame oil
½ teaspoon sugar
Peanut or vegetable oil
1 cup bean sprouts (3 ounces), rinsed, drained, with husks and small bits discarded
1 cup napa cabbage, finely shredded
¼ cup bamboo shoots, cut in matchsticks
¼ cup carrot, cut in matchsticks
¼ cup thinly sliced fresh white or brown mushrooms (2 ounces)
3 scallions (white and green parts), cut in 2-inch lengths and shredded lengthwise
1 garlic clove, minced
1 teaspoon cornstarch dissolved in 1 tablespoon water

Eight 6-inch packaged spring roll or egg roll wrappers, or homemade spring roll wrappers (page 23)
1 tablespoon flour mixed with 1 tablespoon water
Peanut or vegetable oil, for deep-frying

CHOICE OF DIPPING SAUCES
Sweet and Sour Sauce (page 137)
2 tablespoons hoisin sauce mixed with 4 teaspoons water
2 tablespoons plum sauce (see page 134) mixed with 4 teaspoons water
2 teaspoons hot dry mustard, such as Colman's, mixed with 1 tablespoon water

Place the pork and shrimp in separate bowls. In a small bowl, combine the soy sauce, rice wine, sesame oil, and sugar. Pour half the mixture over the pork and half over the shrimp. Mix both well and marinate for 20 minutes.

Heat a wok or nonstick skillet over medium-high heat; then add 2 teaspoons of oil. When it is almost smoking, add the pork and stir-fry for 1 minute; then add the shrimp and cook for 1 minute longer. Transfer the mixture to a large bowl.

Wipe the wok clean with a paper towel, heat, and add 2 more teaspoons of oil. When it is almost smoking, add the bean sprouts, napa cabbage, bamboo shoots, carrot, mushrooms, scallions, and garlic, and cook for 2 minutes, or until crisp-tender. Return the pork and shrimp to the pan; then add the cornstarch mixture and cook for 30 seconds longer, or until the sauce has thickened. Transfer the mixture to the bowl and let it cool. Drain off as much liquid as possible, and then divide the mixture into 8 portions.

Place a wrapper on a flat surface with one corner toward you. Place one portion of the filling diagonally across the wrapper, one third of the way up from the nearest corner, leaving a 1-inch margin on either side. Roll the wrapper away from you

around the filling. Dab a little of the flour mixture on the left and right corners, fold them inward, dab a little flour mixture on the far corner, and finish rolling up the wrapper. Don't roll too tightly or they will not cook through. Place the finished rolls seam side down on a baking sheet. (You may cover and refrigerate the rolls at this point for up to 2 hours.)

Line a baking sheet with several layers of paper towels. Pour 4 to 6 cups of oil in a wok or heavy pot. (The amount of oil you use will depend on the size of your vessel, but the oil should be at least 1½ to 2 inches deep, and no closer than 2 inches to the top.) Clip a candy thermometer to the side of the vessel and heat the oil to 360°F.

Preheat the oven to 200°F.

Carefully lower 2 or 3 spring rolls, one at a time, into the oil. Fry the rolls for 2 to 5 minutes, turning them several times as they cook, until they are evenly golden brown. (Packaged wrappers will cook faster than homemade wrappers; allow about 1 minute longer for refrigerated rolls.) Remove the rolls with a slotted spoon or wire strainer and drain them on the baking sheet. Transfer them to a serving plate and keep them warm in the oven while you cook the remaining rolls. Cut the rolls

crosswise into 3 pieces. Serve hot with
your choice of dipping sauces.

VARIATION
VEGETARIAN SPRING ROLLS

Omit the pork, shrimp, bean sprouts, and
cornstarch mixture. Soak 4 ounces bean
threads (see Note) in hot water for 15
minutes, or until they have softened. Drain
them well, and then cut them into 3-inch
lengths. In a small bowl, combine the soy
sauce, rice wine, sesame oil, and sugar and
set aside. Heat a wok or skillet; then add
1 tablespoon oil. When it is almost smoking, add the napa cabbage, bamboo shoots,
carrot, mushrooms, scallions, and garlic,
and stir-fry for 2 minutes, or until crisp-
tender. Stir in the bean threads and the
soy sauce mixture and cook for 30 seconds
longer. You may also mix in 1 tablespoon
minced fresh cilantro and/or 2 tablespoons chopped dry-roasted peanuts.
Transfer the filling to a bowl and let it
cool. Proceed as above.

NOTE: Bean threads (also called cellophane
noodles or vermicelli) should not be confused
with wheat-based vermicelli or rice noodles.
These clear, wiry noodles are made from
mung bean starch, and sold in dried bundles.

Place filling diagonally

roll

flour mixture

Tuck in sides

flour mixture

BEAN CURD ROLLS

When bean curd sheets are used in place of spring roll wrappers, they make delicately crisp rolls with a slightly nutty flavor. Bean curd rolls may also be steamed after deep-frying, for a soft-textured variation. Any of the dipping sauces for spring rolls (see page 105) can be used for crisp-fried bean curd rolls.

MAKES 8 ROLLS, EACH CUT IN 3 PIECES

4 dried shiitake mushrooms
8 ounces pork shoulder or boneless, skinless chicken (mixture of light and dark meat), coarsely ground
1 grated medium carrot (about ½ cup, lightly packed)
2 scallions (white and green parts), thinly sliced
2 teaspoons crushed or finely minced peeled fresh ginger
1 teaspoon soy sauce
2 teaspoons oyster sauce
½ teaspoon salt
½ teaspoon sugar
1 teaspoon toasted sesame oil
1 teaspoon cornstarch
Bean curd sheets (two 9 × 21-inch sheets [about 9 × 10 inches folded] or four 9 × 11-inch sheets)
1 tablespoon flour mixed with 1 tablespoon water
Peanut or vegetable oil, for deep-frying

Put the shiitake mushrooms in a small bowl and cover them with hot water. Let them stand for 30 to 45 minutes to soften. Drain the mushrooms and cut off and discard the hard stems. Rinse the caps, squeeze them dry, and dice them fine.

In a large bowl, combine the mushrooms, pork, carrot, scallions, ginger, soy sauce, oyster sauce, salt, sugar, sesame oil, and cornstarch. Squeeze the filling through your fingers to blend it well. Let it stand for 30 minutes.

Preheat the oven to 200°F.

Soften the bean curd sheets for 5 minutes in a pan of hot water. Lift the sheets out one at a time to drain off the water, lay them on a flat surface, and pat them dry. Trim off any hard edges; then cut the sheets into rectangles about 8 × 5 inches.

Divide the filling into 8 portions, and shape each one into a 6-inch cylinder. Place one portion diagonally on a bean curd sheet. Roll the bean curd sheet part-way over the filling; then fold the left and right corners inward. Dab a little flour mixture on the far edge, and finish rolling up the bean curd sheet. Place the finished roll seam side down on a baking sheet. Repeat with the remaining ingredients. (You may cover and refrigerate the rolls at this point for up to 2 hours.)

Line a baking sheet with several layers of paper towels. Pour 4 to 6 cups of oil in a wok or heavy pot. (The amount of oil you use will depend on the size of your vessel, but the oil should be at least 1½ to 2 inches deep, and no closer than 2 inches to the top.) Clip a candy thermometer to the side of the vessel and heat the oil to 350°F. Carefully lower 3 or 4 rolls, one at a time, into the oil. Fry the rolls for 2 to 3 minutes, turning them to brown evenly. Remove one roll and cut it crosswise to make sure the filling is cooked through. Remove the rolls with a slotted spoon or wire strainer and drain them on the baking sheet. Transfer them to a serving plate and keep warm in the oven while you cook the remaining rolls. Cut the rolls in thirds crosswise and serve hot.

VARIATION

To make soft bean curd rolls, steam the uncut deep-fried rolls for 5 to 6 minutes over high heat, or until the bean curd sheets are soft. Cut the rolls in thirds crosswise and serve hot.

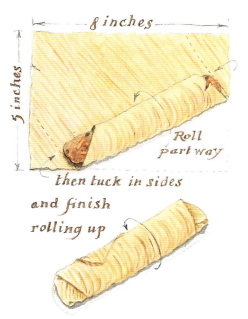

8 inches

5 inches

Roll
part way

then tuck in sides
and finish
rolling up

MOCK CHICKEN

This clever imitation of sliced roast chicken is made almost entirely from bean curd sheets. A soy sauce mixture glazes the outside "skin," and shiitake mushrooms stand in for "bones" when the roll is sliced. Although a restaurant might deep-fry this dish before steaming it, deep-frying such a large roll at home can be tricky. I prefer it simply steamed because it is both lighter in flavor and easier to prepare. The roll can also be made a day ahead and served cold.

MAKES 1 ROLL (SIXTEEN ½-INCH SLICES)

4 to 5 dried shiitake mushrooms (optional)
5 to 6 bean curd sheets (one 6-ounce package)
2 tablespoons soy sauce
1 teaspoon rice wine or dry sherry
1½ teaspoons sugar
⅛ teaspoon ground white pepper
2 teaspoons toasted sesame oil
½ teaspoon salt
2 teaspoons crushed or finely minced peeled fresh ginger

If using, put the shiitake mushrooms in a small bowl and cover them with hot water. Let them stand for 30 to 45 minutes to soften. Drain the mushrooms and cut off and discard the hard stems. Rinse the caps, squeeze them dry, and cut them into ¼-inch slices.

In a large bowl or pan, soak the bean curd sheets in enough hot water to cover for about 5 minutes, or until they become soft. If the bean curd sheets feel very tough after soaking, place them with their soaking water in a large pot. Bring the water to a boil; reduce the heat to low, and cook for 5 minutes, or until tender. Drain the sheets in a colander, rinse gently under cold water, and drain again.

In a small saucepan, mix 2 tablespoons water, the soy sauce, rice wine, sugar, white pepper, sesame oil, salt, and ginger. Bring the sauce to a boil; then reduce the heat to low and cook for 2 minutes. Strain the sauce through a sieve.

Lay one bean curd sheet on a flat sur-

face, pat it gently with a paper towel to dry it, and brush it with the sauce. Set aside the most intact sheet; then stack the remaining sheets on top of the first sheet, one at a time, patting each one dry and then brushing it with the sauce, and trimming the edges to about 9 × 11 inches. Place any scraps between the layers. Starting from a long edge, roll the stack into a tight cylinder. Lay the reserved sheet flat; then place the roll down the center lengthwise. Arrange the sliced mushrooms lengthwise on top of the roll, and wrap the flat sheet around the roll. Place the roll, mushroom side down, on a heat-proof dish. If the roll is too long to fit, cut it in half crosswise. Brush it with the sauce.

Set up a steamer and bring the water to a boil. Steam the roll over high heat for 15 minutes for very soft bean curd sheets, or up to 40 minutes for tougher sheets. Taste a small piece for doneness; it should not be overly chewy. Replenish the steamer with boiling water if necessary.

Meanwhile, put the remaining sauce in a small saucepan and heat it over medium-low heat until it has reduced to about 2 tablespoons. Remove the roll from the steamer. Then pour off any water that may have accumulated in the dish. Brush the top of the roll with the sauce and cool to room temperature. Brush with the sauce again. Cut the roll crosswise into ½-inch-wide slices. Serve at room temperature.

BEAN CURD SHEETS

Bean curd sheets are an inexpensive, nutritious, and versatile product made by skimming off the skin that forms on boiling soy milk, then drying it on mats or poles into brittle sheets. Note that different brands will vary in size from about 8 × 9 inches up to 9 × 21 inches (about 9 × 10 inches folded) or more, and they will also vary widely in chewiness and body. Some will barely hold together after a brief soaking in hot water, while others will still feel quite tough after 10 minutes. Vary cooking times accordingly.

Look for sheets that are relatively intact, because thin sheets are prone to break with too much handling.

MEATS

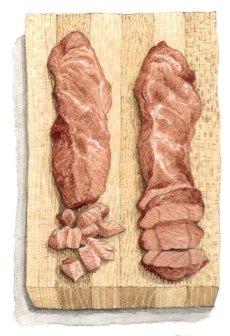

CHAR SIU

My father once recounted a memory of his boyhood in China. During a Japanese occupation, villagers, including his family, were forced to flee to nearby fields, abandoning their homes and possessions. Food was scarce. One night, however, a few villagers risked their lives to return to the village to herd some pigs out to supply pork for all.

Pork does seem to hold a special place in Chinese cooking. It is by far the most commonly used meat in dim sum cooking. The best cut is pork shoulder, and I also like country-style ribs, preferably boneless; both have a good bit of fat for flavor and to keep fillings from becoming too dry. Besides combining pork with many vegetables and seafood for fillings, it may be served straight, marinated and roasted as char siu. Pork spareribs are steamed with chili peppers and black beans.

Beef is seen less on the dim sum cart, but it is sometimes found in meatballs on a bed of watercress or bean curd sheets. It is also stewed with star anise, and organ meats such as tripe may be added.

Other meat and poultry dishes bear at least a mention. You might feel adventurous enough some time to sample stewed pork liver, cubes of blood pudding, sweet-vinegared pigs' feet, sliced roast duck, or braised chicken feet or duck webs. There are those who believe fondness for chicken feet distinguishes a true dim sum fan. Although I have not included recipes for these more esoteric plates, give them a try at your next dim sum outing.

CHAR SIU

Char siu, strips of marinated, roasted pork, makes a fine dim sum dish on its own, cut crosswise into thin slices. More often, though, it is the basis for fillings for other dishes such as steamed or baked buns, or savory pastries. You can also toss it into stir-fried vegetables, or dice or sliver it as a topping over rice and other dishes. I can never resist popping a few pieces in my mouth when I cook with it.

In Chinatown, char siu is readily available—you'll see it hanging alongside roast chickens and ducks in every storefront window. If you are not near a Chinatown, however, or would prefer to make your own, here's a simple recipe, adapted from Every Grain of Rice. *(Illustrated on page 112.)*

MAKES 1 TO 1½ POUNDS

½ teaspoon curing salt (see Note)
¼ cup hoisin sauce
¼ cup ketchup
¼ cup honey, plus 2 tablespoons for
    glazing
1½ to 2 pounds boneless country-style
    spareribs, cut to 6 × 1 × 1½ inches

Combine the curing salt, hoisin sauce, ketchup, and ¼ cup honey in a baking dish. Add the pork, turning the pieces to coat them evenly with the marinade; then cover and refrigerate for 3 hours.

Preheat the oven to 400°F.

Place the meat on an oiled, perforated broiling pan, and bake for 25 to 30 minutes, or until cooked through. While the pork is still hot, brush it with additional honey. Broil the pork for 2 to 3 minutes on each side, and then brush it again with honey. Let the pork rest for several minutes before slicing it. Leftover char siu may be cooled, wrapped, and refrigerated for up to 3 days or frozen for up to a month.

NOTE: Curing salt, also known as sodium nitrite or saltpeter, gives char siu its characteristic texture and pink color. If you cannot find it or prefer not to use it, substitute 1 teaspoon salt.

STEAMED SPARERIBS

My mother claims steamed spareribs are more tender and flavorful when made a day ahead. All the last-minute attention they need is a quick steaming to heat them through.

MAKES 6 TO 8 SERVINGS AS PART OF A DIM SUM MEAL

1 pound pork spareribs
1 tablespoon cornstarch
1 teaspoon fermented black beans, rinsed and drained
3 dried hot chilies, seeded and crumbled
2 garlic cloves, finely minced
1 teaspoon soy sauce
1 teaspoon salt
2 teaspoons rice wine or dry sherry
¼ teaspoon sugar

Cut the spareribs apart and chop crosswise into 1-inch pieces. (You may prefer to have the butcher do this.) Place them in a bowl and toss with the cornstarch.

In a small bowl, combine the fermented black beans, chilies, garlic, soy sauce, salt, rice wine, and sugar; then pour the mixture over the spareribs, cover, and refrigerate for 1 hour.

Set up a steamer and bring the water to a boil. Transfer the spareribs to a heatproof plate and steam over high heat for 30 to 40 minutes, or until tender. Check the water level in the steamer occasionally and replenish it with boiling water if necessary. Remove the spareribs from the heat.

Skim off and discard the fat from the sauce before serving. Serve hot.

(You may let the spareribs cool, cover, and refrigerate them overnight. Skim off and discard the hardened fat from the sauce, and steam the spareribs over high heat for 4 to 5 minutes, or until they are heated through.)

BEEF MEATBALLS

Beef meatballs, seasoned with tangerine peel and served on a bed of bean curd sheets or watercress, are a dim sum standby. I like the coarser texture of hand-chopped beef, but you may use ground beef if you prefer.

MAKES ABOUT 14 MEATBALLS

1 teaspoon dried tangerine peel (optional; see Note)
1 pound beef, chopped or ground
1 teaspoon baking soda
2 teaspoons rice wine or dry sherry
1 large egg white, lightly beaten
2 teaspoons soy sauce
1 tablespoon oyster sauce
½ teaspoon salt
½ teaspoon sugar
⅛ teaspoon ground white pepper
1 teaspoon toasted sesame oil
1 tablespoon peanut or vegetable oil
1 tablespoon cornstarch
3 bean curd sheets or 4 bean curd sticks

If using the dried tangerine peel, put it in a small bowl and cover it with hot water. Let it stand for 30 minutes to soften.

In a large bowl, combine the beef and the baking soda. Squeeze the mixture through your fingers to blend it well. Let it stand for 30 minutes at room temperature.

Drain and then mince the tangerine peel. Add it to the beef with the rice wine, beaten egg white, and ¼ cup water, and squeeze the mixture through your fingers again.

In a small bowl, mix the soy sauce, oyster sauce, salt, sugar, white pepper, sesame oil, peanut oil, and cornstarch. Add the ingredients to the beef, and squeeze the mixture through your fingers again. This process will help the beef hold together when it is cooked. Let it stand for 30 minutes at room temperature.

Meanwhile, if using bean curd sheets, place them in a pan with enough hot water to cover them and soak for 5 minutes, or until soft; then shake off the water. If using bean curd sticks, break them in half, place them in a bowl with enough hot water to

TO CHOP OR TO GRIND?

When food processors first became popular, one older aunt insisted her hand-chopped meat was superior to what the appliance could produce. I remember thinking that she seemed hopelessly old-fashioned, but I have since come to agree with her.

A sharp cleaver and a stable wooden chopping block make quick work of chopping the small quantity of meat required for most dim sum dishes. Cut the meat into 1-inch cubes before chopping it, and slide the cleaver blade under the meat from time to time to turn it over and keep it in a compact mass. What I especially like about this technique is that it is almost impossible to chop the meat too fine accidentally. Compare this with the split-second attention required not to overprocess meat in the food processor. Besides, if you add the time it takes to assemble the food processor and wash all its components, the overall difference in preparation time is negligible.

cover them, and soak for 20 minutes, or until soft. Cut off and discard any hard ends, and squeeze out the water. Line one large or several small heat-proof plates with the bean curd sheets or sticks, cutting them to fit if necessary.

Lightly shape the beef into meatballs, using about 2 tablespoons of beef for each one. Place them slightly apart on the bean curd sheets or sticks.

Set up a steamer and bring the water to a boil. Steam the meatballs for 8 minutes over high heat, or until cooked through. Serve hot.

NOTE: Dried tangerine peel gives this dish its characteristic flavor. However, it is fairly strong, so you may prefer to omit it. If you cannot find dried tangerine peel you may dry your own by leaving a whole tangerine peel on a plate in a warm, dry place for a week, until it becomes dark and leathery. You may also substitute 1 teaspoon minced fresh tangerine or orange zest, using the colored part only.

VARIATIONS

✦ Replace the bean curd sheets or sticks with 1 bunch of watercress. Discard any large, tough stems, and line the heat-proof plates with the watercress.
✦ Add 3 tablespoons minced water chestnuts to the meat with the seasonings. Omit the dried tangerine peel.

BEEF STEW

Some dim sum carts are designed just for stews to be ladled out piping hot at your table; their divided metal bins hold beef, tripe, other organ meats, beef tendon, and cubes of blood pudding. My favorite is a simple beef stew, almost always flavored with star anise. Homemade stew is even better if you make it a day or two ahead. Toss in some root vegetables—carrots, chunks of daikon radish, or potatoes—for a complete meal. Tripe fans should note the tripe variation requires slightly longer cooking; it also benefits from being made ahead and reheated.

MAKES 6 TO 8 SERVINGS AS PART OF A DIM SUM
MEAL, OR 4 TO 6 SERVINGS AS AN ENTRÉE

1 tablespoon peanut or vegetable oil
1 onion, halved, then thinly sliced
    crosswise
2 pounds beef stew meat (or part beef
    shank meat), cut in 1½-inch cubes
1-inch piece of fresh ginger, peeled and
    halved
1 tablespoon red bean curd (optional; see
    Note), or 1 teaspoon salt
3 to 4 whole star anise
2 teaspoons soy sauce
2 teaspoons rice wine or dry sherry
1 medium carrot, cut diagonally in ½-inch
    thick pieces (optional)
1 cup daikon radish (5 ounces), peeled and
    cut in 1-inch cubes (optional)

2 boiling potatoes (6 to 8 ounces), peeled
    and cut in 1-inch chunks (optional)
1 tablespoon cornstarch dissolved in
    1 tablespoon water

Heat a heavy dutch oven over medium-high heat; then add the oil. When it is almost smoking, add the onion and stir-fry for 2 minutes. Add the beef, ginger, and red bean curd, and stir-fry for 8 minutes longer, or until the meat is browned.

    Add the star anise, soy sauce, and rice wine, and enough water to almost cover the meat. Bring to a boil; then reduce the

heat to low, cover, and cook for 2 to 2½ hours, or until the meat is tender. If using carrot, daikon radish, and/or potatoes, add them for the last 20 to 25 minutes of cooking. Discard the ginger and star anise.

Stir in the cornstarch mixture and cook for 1 minute longer, or until the sauce has thickened.

This stew may be cooled, covered, and refrigerated for up to 2 days. It may also be made ahead without the vegetables, covered, and frozen. Thaw the stew, and then reheat it over medium heat for 10 minutes, or until bubbly. Reduce the heat to low, add the vegetables, and cook as above.

NOTE: Sold in jars, red bean curd is made from blocks of soybean curd fermented in wine, red rice, and salt. It has a pungent, salty flavor, and is used sparingly as a seasoning or marinade ingredient. It will keep indefinitely refrigerated.

VARIATION
TRIPE STEW

Replace the beef stew meat with beef tripe. Omit the onion and oil. Rinse the tripe well, and then cut it into ½ × 2½-inch strips. In a large pot, bring 6 cups of water to a boil. Reduce the heat to medium, and add the tripe. Cook for 2 minutes, or until the water returns to a boil. Pour the tripe into a colander and rinse it under cold water.

Put the tripe in a heavy pot with 4 cups of water, the ginger, red bean curd, star anise, soy sauce, and rice wine. Cover the pot, bring the liquid to a boil over medium-high heat, and then reduce the heat to low and cook for 3 hours, or until the tripe is tender. Add a little water from time to time if necessary. Discard the ginger and star anise. Stir in the cornstarch mixture and cook for 1 minute longer, or until the sauce has thickened.

STAR ANISE

SWEETS

BAKED SWEET BAO

Desserts are not typically served at the end of a Chinese meal, but sweets are de rigueur on dim sum carts. Selections range from cool cubes of almond pudding to flaky tarts to deep-fried sugar puffs. As with savory dim sum, sweets may be steamed, deep-fried, pan-fried, or baked. Ingredients include custard, coconut, nuts, lotus seeds, sesame seeds, and sweet bean paste. Vanilla finds its way into some sweets, but rarely butter or other dairy products, and never chocolate.

It's not necessary to order a sweet to finish lunch, or to offer any if you are planning a menu at home, but a light dessert or two does add welcome variety, and most are not overly sweet.

ALMOND PUDDING

Cubes of this simple, light pudding refresh the palate at the end of a meal, and it is enhanced by a little fruit for color. You can find it on many dim sum carts, and it might be garnished with canned fruit cocktail or paper parasols to catch the eyes of children. This was originally made with agar agar, a seaweed, but unflavored gelatin is more readily available and yields similar results.

MAKES 8 SERVINGS

½ cup sugar
2 tablespoons unflavored gelatin
  (two ¼-ounce packages)
1½ cups milk
2 teaspoons almond extract
About 2 cups mixed fruit, such as lychees,
  sliced kiwis, diced mango, and grapes

Combine 2 cups water and the sugar in a saucepan. Sprinkle the gelatin over the mixture and let it stand for 5 minutes, or until softened. Heat the mixture over low heat for 5 to 6 minutes, stirring to dissolve the sugar and gelatin. Remove the mixture from the heat. Stir in the milk and almond extract.

Pour the mixture into a 9-inch square pan, cover, and refrigerate for 2 to 3 hours, or until set. (You may also divide the mixture into 8 small bowls and serve the pudding right from the bowls.) Cut the pudding into 1-inch cubes and transfer them to individual bowls. Garnish with the fruit and serve cold.

MANGO PUDDING

This pretty, refreshing pudding is showing up in various forms on dessert carts of late. It might be garnished with whipped cream, and I've also seen it with a mysterious accompaniment of evaporated milk on the side. Some mango puddings contain tapioca, agar agar, or coconut milk. This creamy version is very simple; I like it topped with slices of fresh mango or other fruit. A variation using part coconut milk follows.

MAKES 8 SERVINGS

½ cup water plus 1¾ cups boiling water
2 tablespoons unflavored gelatin
   (2 envelopes)
1¼ cups sugar
2 mangoes
1 cup half-and-half
Fruit for garnishes, such as kiwi, grapes, or
   tangerine segments

Put the ½ cup water in a large bowl. Sprinkle the gelatin over the water and let it stand for 5 minutes, or until softened. Add the boiling water, and stir to dissolve the gelatin; then immediately stir in the sugar. Set aside.

    Peel the mangoes and cut the flesh off the pits. Reserve half of one mango for garnish, and cut the remaining mango into chunks, then process it in a food processor to make a smooth purée. You should have about 2 cups puréed mango. Stir the purée into the gelatin mixture, and then stir in the half-and-half.

    Divide the mixture among 8 individual bowls and refrigerate it for 3 hours, or until set. Top the pudding with sliced mango or other fruit.

VARIATIONS

+ For a firmer, less creamy-textured pudding, use 3 tablespoons unflavored gelatin. This version may be chilled in a 9 × 13-inch pan and cut in squares once it has set. It may also be put in decorative molds; once it has set, place them for a few seconds in a pan of hot water that reaches almost all the way up the sides of the molds. Invert the molds on individual dishes and garnish as desired.
+ For coconut mango pudding, reduce the quantity of boiling water to 1½ cups. Add ¾ cup coconut milk with ½ cup half-and-half.

BAKED SWEET BAO

These sweet buns use the same dough and cooking techniques as savory baked char siu bao. They usually enclose a bit of sweet lotus or sweet red bean filling, although some restaurants fill the buns with custard or coconut and chopped peanuts. (Illustrated on page 120.)

MAKES THIRTY-SIX 2½-INCH BUNS

Baked Char Siu Bao dough (see page 58)
1 cup Sweet Lotus Filling (see page 124)
   or Sweet Red Bean Filling (see page 125)
1 large egg, beaten

Oil 2 baking sheets and set them aside.

Punch down the risen dough, and turn it out onto a well-floured board. Roll it out to a 12 × 12-inch square and cut it into thirty-six 2-inch squares, 6 across and 6 down.

Hold a portion of dough on one palm and flatten it with your fingers into a 2¼-inch circle, slightly thicker in the middle than around the edges. Place a barely rounded teaspoon of filling onto the center. Gather the edges of the dough together and pinch firmly to seal in the filling completely.

Put the bun, pinched side down, on an oiled baking sheet. Repeat with the remaining dough and filling, spacing finished buns 2 inches apart. Cover the buns loosely with plastic wrap, and let them rise in a warm, draft-free place for 30 minutes.

Preheat the oven to 350°F.

With a pastry brush, brush the buns lightly with the beaten egg.

Bake the buns for 20 to 25 minutes, or until golden brown. To check for doneness, tear a bun in half; the bread should be airy rather than raw-looking and doughy.

Transfer the buns to a wire rack to cool slightly before serving. Mark the tops with a red dot as for Steamed Sweet Bao (page 124) while the buns are still hot.

Once they have cooled completely, the buns may be covered and refrigerated for up to 24 hours. Let the buns reach room temperature, and then reheat them for 5 to 7 minutes in a 350°F. oven, or until they are heated through.

These buns also freeze well. Let them thaw completely; then reheat as above.

STEAMED SWEET BAO

The most popular filling for sweet bao is made from lotus seeds, extracted from the pods of water lily flowers. The seeds are simmered with sugar until they reduce to a paste with a sublime, almost flowery flavor.

Also popular is a filling made from sweetened adzuki beans. It cooks down to a thick, dark paste with a rich, brown sugar flavor.

Either filling yields twice what you need here, but if you make less, both are prone to burn or dry out before they reach the right consistency. Both fillings can also be used for Baked Sweet Bao (page 123), and both freeze well.

For a traditional touch, mark finished sweet bao with a red dot to differentiate them from bao with savory fillings. Mix 2 drops of red food coloring with a few drops of water. Dip the end of a chopstick into the food coloring; then lightly touch the center of the hot buns with it.

MAKES 24 BUNS

SWEET LOTUS FILLING
6 ounces lotus seeds (about 1⅓ cups dried)
1½ cups sugar
3 tablespoons peanut or vegetable oil

Steamed Bao Dough (page 53)

Rinse the lotus seeds in a colander. Place them in a large bowl with 5 cups of water, and let them soak for 2 hours or overnight. Open the seeds; then discard any bitter green buds inside. Place the seeds in a heavy saucepan with 3 cups of fresh water and bring to a boil. Reduce the heat to low and cook, covered, for 2½ to 3 hours, or until tender. Stir occasionally at first and then more frequently toward the end of the cooking time. Add a little water as necessary to prevent the seeds from burning. The lotus seeds will become very mushy. Pour the mixture into a food processor or blender and process until smooth. Return the mixture to the saucepan.

Stir in the sugar and oil and cook the mixture for 30 to 35 minutes, uncovered, over medium-low heat, stirring frequently, and reducing the heat if the mixture begins to scorch. It should become slightly translucent

SWEET LOTUS BAO

and quite thick. Measure out 1 cup of the filling; reserve the remainder for another use. (You may cover and refrigerate the filling for up to 2 days, or freeze it for up to 1 month.)

Line a steamer basket (see page 17) or metal steamer tiers with several layers of dampened cheesecloth. Cut twenty-four 2-inch squares of baking parchment.

Divide the filling into 24 portions. Divide the dough into 24 pieces. Use your fingertips to lightly flatten one piece of dough into a 3½-inch circle and place the circle flat on one palm. Put one portion of the filling onto the center; then gather the edges of the dough together and pinch tightly. Place the bun pinched side down on a square of parchment, and place it in a prepared steamer tier. Repeat with the remaining dough and filling, spacing the buns 1 inch apart in the steamer tiers. Stack the tiers (excluding the steamer bottom), covering the top tier loosely with plastic wrap. Let the buns rise for 30 minutes. You will have to steam the buns in 2 or 3 batches.

Bring the water in the steamer to a boil over high heat. Steam a single tier of buns at a time over high heat for 12 minutes, replenishing the pot with water as necessary between batches. Serve hot.

Cooled buns may be sealed in a plastic bag, and either refrigerated for several days or frozen for up to a month. Thaw the buns before reheating them; then steam them for 5 to 6 minutes.

VARIATION
SWEET RED BEAN FILLING

1 cup adzuki beans
½ cup peanut or vegetable oil
1 cup brown sugar, packed

Adzuki Beans

Wash and drain the adzuki beans. Place them in a bowl with 2 cups of water and let them soak overnight. Drain them, and then place them in a large saucepan with 3 cups of fresh water. Bring the water to a boil; then reduce the heat to low, and cook, covered, for about 1½ hours, or until the beans are tender. Process the beans through a food mill to remove the skins. Discard the skins and return the puréed beans to the saucepan. Stir in the oil and brown sugar.

Cook over low heat, uncovered, stirring frequently, for 45 to 50 minutes, or until the mixture is very thick. Transfer the filling to a bowl, cover, and refrigerate for up to 2 days. Measure out 1 cup of the filling; reserve the remainder for another use. (You may cover and refrigerate the filling for up to 2 days, or freeze it for up to 1 month.) Substitute the filling for the sweet lotus filling, and proceed as above.

COCONUT BALLS

If you're familiar with Japanese mochi, *you'll recognize the flavors and texture of these pleasantly sticky sweets. The snowy coconut balls combine the chewiness of boiled glutinous rice flour dough with the smoothness of lotus seed filling. The coconut coating adds yet another contrasting texture.*

MAKES 12 COCONUT BALLS

1½ cups glutinous rice flour, plus
    additional for dusting the board
1 teaspoon peanut or vegetable oil
½ cup Sweet Lotus Filling (see page 124) or
    Sweet Red Bean Filling (see page 125)
About ¾ cup flaked unsweetened coconut,
    lightly packed

In a large bowl, combine the glutinous rice flour, oil, and ¾ cup water; add a few more drops of water at a time, if necessary, until the dough holds together. Squeeze the dough through your fingers to blend it well; it should be slightly sticky, not dry. Divide the dough into 12 pieces.

Flatten one piece of dough into a 2½-inch circle, slightly thicker in the center than around the edges. Place 1 teaspoon of the filling onto the center, gather the edges of the dough together, and pinch firmly to seal in the filling completely. Wet your hands, and then roll the dough into a smooth ball between your palms. Place the ball on a large plate. Repeat with the remaining ingredients.

Oil a baking sheet and set aside.

In a large saucepan, bring 6 cups of water to a boil. Drop the balls, one at a time, into the water. Stir them gently with a wooden spoon to separate and prevent them from sticking to the pan. Cook the balls over medium-high heat for 5 to 6 minutes, or until they float to the surface and are cooked through. Remove the balls

COCONUT BALLS

with a slotted spoon and place them on the baking sheet. Turn off the heat, but leave the water in the saucepan.

Put about ⅓ cup of the coconut in a small dish. While the balls are still hot, roll them, one at a time, in the coconut. If the balls begin to dry out, immerse them briefly in the hot water in the saucepan; then remove them with a slotted spoon, and roll them in the coconut. Add coconut to the plate as needed. Arrange the finished balls on a serving plate. Serve at room temperature.

VARIATIONS

✦ Replace the coconut with ½ cup very finely chopped unsalted dry-roasted peanuts mixed with 2 tablespoons sugar. The peanuts must be chopped fine with a sharp knife or cleaver; do not grind them in a food processor or blender, because grinding will release oils and turn the peanuts into peanut butter.

✦ Replace the filling with a mixture of ¼ cup finely chopped unsalted dry-roasted peanuts, 1 tablespoon flaked unsweetened coconut, and 1 tablespoon sugar. Heat a skillet over medium heat; then add 2 teaspoons oil. When hot, add the mixture and stir-fry for 2½ to 3 minutes, or until the coconut is slightly toasted. Cool the filling to room temperature. Use 1 heaping teaspoon of the filling for each ball, and proceed as above.

EGG CUSTARD TARTS

Every restaurant offers these don tot, but for such a simple item, they vary tremendously; some are so small they hold little more than a thimbleful of custard, while others have thick—and sometimes undercooked—multi-layered crusts. I like these thin shells because they bake to a delicate crispness, and they are sized to hold an ample portion of filling.

Handle the dough lightly and quickly, taking care not to overwork it or it will become tough. A perfect 3¼-inch cutter can be made from a washed tuna or bamboo-shoot can with both ends removed. The tart shells may be made ahead and frozen, so that finishing the tarts is very quick and easy. Keeping the oven temperature low prevents the custard filling from becoming watery or tough.

MAKES 12 TARTS

TART SHELLS
1 cup unsifted all-purpose flour
1 tablespoon sugar
¼ cup vegetable shortening or lard
¼ cup ice water, plus a few teaspoons
   additional

FILLING
2 large eggs
½ cup sugar
½ cup milk
½ teaspoon vanilla extract

TO MAKE THE TART SHELLS In a large bowl, sift together the flour and sugar. Cut in the shortening with a pastry blender or two knives, until the shortening is the size of almonds. With a few quick squeezes between your fingers and thumbs, flatten the pieces of shortening in the flour. Stir the ice water into the flour mixture with a fork, until the dough barely holds together. Add a few drops more water if necessary, but do not overwork the dough. Press the dough into a ball, cover it with plastic wrap, and flatten it into a 6-inch square. Refrigerate the dough for 2 hours.

On a lightly floured board, roll the dough to a 10 × 13-inch rectangle. With a cookie cutter, cut twelve 3¼-inch circles. Fit the circles into 12 ungreased 3¼-inch fluted tart tins or a muffin tin, pressing the dough lightly into the bottom. Refrigerate the tart shells while you prepare the filling. (At this point, you may cover and freeze the tart shells for up to 1 month. Let the tart shells thaw for 30 minutes before filling them.)

Preheat the oven to 325°F.

TO MAKE THE FILLING In a medium bowl, beat the eggs, sugar, milk, and vanilla. Let the mixture rest for 15 minutes; then skim off any bubbles. Spoon the mixture evenly into the unbaked tart shells. Bake for 30 to 35 minutes, or until a knife inserted in the center of a tart comes out clean and the crusts are lightly browned.

Cool the tarts for 5 minutes, use a knife or spatula to loosen the tarts, and transfer them to a wire rack to cool completely. Serve at room temperature. Refrigerate leftover tarts.

EGG CUSTARD TART

COCONUT WALNUT TART

COCONUT WALNUT TARTS

A close cousin to egg custard tarts, these sweets have a macaroon-like coconut filling studded with chopped nuts. Make the tart shells and chill them before you prepare the filling.

MAKES 12 TARTS

1 tablespoon butter
½ cup sugar
2 large eggs
½ cup milk
¾ cup unsweetened shredded or flaked coconut, lightly packed
¼ cup finely chopped walnuts
12 unbaked tart shells (see page 128)

Preheat the oven to 400°F.

In a medium bowl, cream the butter and sugar with an electric mixer at medium speed. Add the eggs and milk, and continue beating until the mixture is well blended. Stir in the coconut and walnuts.

Spoon the mixture evenly into the unbaked tart shells. Bake for 25 to 30 minutes, or until the filling is set and the crusts are lightly browned. Cool for 5 minutes; then use a knife or spatula to loosen the tarts and transfer them to a wire rack to cool completely. Refrigerate leftover tarts.

SWEET RED BEAN–FILLED PANCAKES

Originating from northern China, these crepe-like pancakes enclose the same sweet red bean filling used for steamed or baked buns. This dish is sometimes deep-fried, but pan-frying is easier.

MAKES 4 PANCAKES, EACH CUT IN 6 PIECES

2 large eggs
¾ cup sifted all-purpose flour
1 tablespoon peanut or vegetable oil, plus
    additional for the pan
1 cup Sweet Red Bean Filling (see
    page 125)
1 tablespoon flour mixed with
    1 tablespoon water
Superfine sugar, for sprinkling pancakes
    (optional)

In a large bowl, whisk the eggs with ¾ cup water until well blended. Whisk in the flour; then whisk in the tablespoon of oil. The batter will have a few very small lumps. Cover and let it stand for 20 minutes.

Heat a 10-inch nonstick skillet or crepe pan over medium-low heat. Add a teaspoon of oil and wipe it evenly around the skillet with a paper towel.

Measure just over ⅓ cup batter into a measuring cup. Pour the batter into the skillet, lift the skillet off the burner, and quickly tilt it all around to spread the batter into an 8-inch circle. (If the batter sets before you can spread it around, reduce the heat.) Cook for 1 minute, or until the pancake turns dry around the edges and is no longer shiny in the center. Lift an edge carefully to check for doneness; the pancake should look dry but not brown. Loosen the pancake with a spatula and

RED BEAN–FILLED PANCAKES

slide it onto a plate. Repeat the procedure with the remaining batter, making 4 pancakes in all and stacking the finished pancakes. (At this point, the pancakes may be cooled, covered with plastic wrap, and refrigerated for up to 24 hours.)

Spread ¼ cup sweet red bean filling in a 2-inch-wide strip down the length of each pancake, just left of the center. Dab a little flour mixture around the edge to the right of the center. Roll the pancake, starting from the left, to make a flattened cylinder. Press the edge lightly to seal in the filling.

Heat the skillet over medium-high heat, and then add 2 tablespoons of oil. When it is almost smoking, cook 1 or 2 filled pancakes at a time for 1 to 2 minutes, or until browned, then turn them over and cook 1 to 2 minutes longer to brown the other side, adding oil as necessary.

Place several layers of paper towels on a plate. Drain the pancakes on the paper towels while you pan-fry the remaining pancakes. Transfer the finished pancakes to a serving plate; then cut each crosswise into 6 pieces. If desired, you may sprinkle the pancakes lightly with superfine sugar. Serve hot.

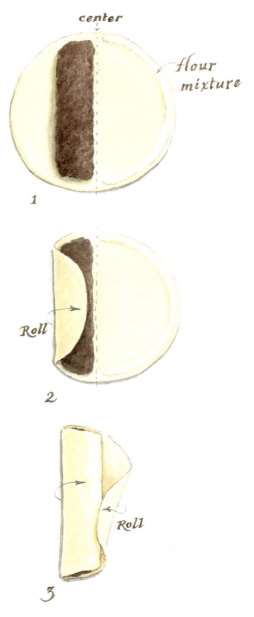

SUGAR PUFFS

Sugar puffs split and expand dramatically as they fry. Despite their name, their only sweetness comes from a light dusting of superfine sugar. They are best served hot, but then I rarely have any left by the time they would have cooled.

MAKES ABOUT 16 PUFFS

1½ cups all-purpose flour
1½ teaspoons baking powder
1 cup boiling water
2 large eggs
About ¼ cup superfine sugar
Peanut or vegetable oil, for deep-frying

Sift the flour and baking powder into a large bowl. Add the boiling water all at once, stirring until the dough is well blended and very thick. Let it cool for 5 minutes; then add the eggs, one at a time, squeezing the mixture through your fingers to make a thick, sticky dough.

Line a baking sheet with several layers of paper towels. Place 2 tablespoons of the superfine sugar in a small paper bag.

Pour 4 to 6 cups of oil in a wok or heavy pot. (The amount of oil you use will depend on the size of your vessel, but the oil should be at least 1½ to 2 inches deep, and no closer than 2 inches to the top.) Clip a candy thermometer to the side of the vessel and heat the oil to 325°F.

Wet a tablespoon and your hands. Scoop a rounded tablespoon of dough; then remove it from the spoon with your hands and roll it lightly into a ball. Drop it carefully into the oil. Repeat the procedure, cooking 4 puffs at a time. Rotate the puffs with a slotted spoon to separate them and prevent them from sticking to the pot. Keep the oil temperature between 310°F. and 330°F.; if the oil overheats the puffs will not expand properly. They should begin to split open after 3 to 4 minutes. Cook for 7 minutes, or until golden brown.

Remove the puffs with a slotted spoon or wire strainer and drain them on the baking sheets. While they are still hot, put a batch of the puffs in the paper bag with the sugar and shake gently to coat. Repeat with each batch, replenishing the bag with sugar as necessary. Serve hot or at room temperature.

SAUCES
AND
CONDIMENTS

CHILI OIL

chili Pepper

PLUM SAUCE

PEPPERSALT with Chinese Five-Spice Powder

SOY VINEGAR DIP

Scallions

Szechuan Peppercorns

SWEET AND SOUR SAUCE

HOT MUSTARD

SWEET SOY SAUCE

SAUCES AND CONDIMENTS

At dim sum restaurants, tables may or may not be set with a few bottles or dishes of condiments and sauces, but a properly seasoned dumpling should not require an immediate dousing in soy sauce. Outside the West, restaurants don't provide straight soy sauce at all, and your waitress will only set condiments on the table as appropriate to a particular dish you have ordered. These may include peppersalt, hot mustard, chili oil or chili paste, sweet and sour sauce, red vinegar, or soy sauce mixtures with vinegar, ginger, scallions, or sugar. These enhancements are not meant to add saltiness; rather they add another dimension of flavor to an already well-seasoned mouthful.

HOT MUSTARD

In addition to chili oil, hot mustard is often provided as a standard condiment. In our house, this always meant Colman's dry mustard, stirred into a paste with a few drops of water. I have often seen people mixing mustard into soy sauce on their plates. I don't know if this is proper etiquette, though I suspect it is not.

If you are going to use mustard, try Colman's for its hot, clean flavor, and remember that a little goes a very long way. Numerous prepared hot Chinese mustards are available; avoid ball-park or Dijon mustards

PLUM SAUCE

A tangy alternative to sweet and sour sauce is plum sauce. Sold in jars, it is made from plums mixed with sugar, vinegar, salt, ginger, chili, and garlic, and it tastes similar to some prepared chutneys. It may be used as is or thinned first with a few drops of water.

PEPPERSALT WITH CHINESE FIVE-SPICE POWDER

I'm convinced it's the peppersalt that makes Salt-Fried Whole Prawns (page 104) impossible to resist. The spices in Chinese five-spice powder—cinnamon, star anise, fennel, Szechuan peppercorns, and cloves—round out the heat of the pepper and sharpness of the salt. Use Szechuan peppercorns if you can find them; they are actually from a different plant family than white or black peppercorns, and they imbue the peppersalt with a distinct fragrance.

Besides being used as a seasoning, small dishes of peppersalt may be provided for dipping fried squab or chicken. Try sprinkling peppersalt on hard-boiled eggs or scrambled eggs, or use it in place of salt and pepper.

MAKES 3 TABLESPOONS

1 tablespoon Szechuan peppercorns or
   2 teaspoons ground white pepper
2 tablespoons salt
⅛ teaspoon Chinese five-spice powder

If using Szechuan peppercorns, heat a dry skillet over medium-low heat, and then add the peppercorns. Cook for about 1 minute, shaking the pan gently, until the peppercorns are fragrant and lightly toasted, but not browned. Remove the peppercorns from the skillet and let them cool. In a blender or spice grinder, blend the peppercorns with the salt and Chinese five-spice powder until the mixture has a very fine texture.

If using white pepper, combine it with the salt and Chinese five-spice powder in a blender or spice grinder and blend the mixture until it has a very fine texture.

Heat a dry nonstick skillet over medium-low heat; then add the peppersalt and heat it for about 30 seconds, until it is fragrant. Remove it from the heat and let it cool.

Transfer the peppersalt to a salt shaker, or store the unused portion in an airtight container.

SOY VINEGAR DIP

Potstickers are traditionally accompanied by small dishes of this dip. The tang of sweetened vinegar offsets the crisp crust of a potsticker wrapper and cuts the richness of the pork filling.

MAKES ½ CUP

¼ cup soy sauce
2 tablespoons rice vinegar
2 teaspoons sugar
1 teaspoon scallion (green part only), sliced paper thin

In a small non-aluminum saucepan, combine the soy sauce, rice vinegar, sugar, and 2 tablespoons water, and heat over low heat for 1½ minutes, or until the sugar has dissolved. Remove the sauce from the heat, and spoon it into small dishes for dipping. Sprinkle the sauce with scallions.

The sauce may be covered and refrigerated for up to 2 weeks. Add the scallions just before using.

SWEET SOY SAUCE

A waitress will usually keep a cruet of this diluted, lightly sweetened soy sauce on her cart to pour over your rice flour rolls as soon as you order them.

MAKES ABOUT ⅓ CUP

2 tablespoons soy sauce
1 tablespoon sugar
2 teaspoons toasted sesame oil
2 teaspoons scallion (green part only), sliced paper-thin (optional)

In a small saucepan, combine the soy sauce, sugar, sesame oil, and 3 tablespoons water, and cook over low heat for about 1½ minutes, or until the sugar has dissolved. Remove from the heat and stir in the scallions, if using.

The sauce may be covered and refrigerated for up to 2 weeks. Let it reach room temperature, and add the scallions just before using.

SWEET AND SOUR SAUCE

This sauce goes well with deep-fried crab claws and seaweed-wrapped rolls. It also often accompanies spring rolls.

MAKES 1 SCANT CUP

¼ cup ketchup
¼ cup vinegar, preferably rice or apple cider vinegar
¼ cup firmly packed light or dark brown sugar
1 teaspoon cornstarch dissolved in 1 tablespoon water

In a small, non-aluminum saucepan, combine the ketchup, vinegar, brown sugar, and ¼ cup water. Cook over low heat for 2 to 3 minutes, or until the sugar has dissolved. Raise the heat to medium, and cook the sauce until it begins to boil. Stir in the cornstarch mixture, and continue cooking for 30 seconds, or until the sauce has thickened. Spoon the sauce into small dishes for dipping.

CHILI OIL

Chinese grocery stores stock numerous brands of bottled chili oil, but it's a quick job to make your own, and it will keep for several months at room temperature in an airtight jar. Chili oil may be used as a condiment for many dumplings as well as noodle dishes or soups by those who like a little heat in their food.

MAKES ¾ CUP

¾ cup peanut or vegetable oil
8 to 12 dried red chilies (including seeds), or more to taste, crumbled or cut in ¼-inch pieces
1 garlic clove, peeled (optional)

In a small saucepan, heat the oil for 2½ to 3 minutes over medium heat until it reaches 220°F. Add the chilies and garlic, if using, and cook for 1 minute, or until the garlic is sizzling and just beginning to color. Remove the mixture from the heat and let it cool; then transfer it to a clean, airtight jar. Let the mixture stand for at least 2 to 3 days; then discard the garlic clove. The oil is now ready to use; you may use either just the oil, or include a few chili bits for even hotter flavor.

PLANNING A MENU

If you've experienced the dazzling array of dishes at a dim sum restaurant, it may seem daunting to try duplicating such a spread at home. Planning is essential; the trick is to select some dishes that require little or no last-minute attention—just steaming or baking—so you can pan-fry or deep-fry a dish or two at the same time.

Dim sum combinations are infinite; be sure to offer different meats and seafood rather than having, say, all pork dishes. Consider color, texture, and shape, too, because dim sum is also a feast for the eyes.

These six sample menus include something light to make ahead and re-steam, something crisp or fried for a little richness, something starchy to stick to your ribs, something green, and a sweet.

Many of the dishes may be made ahead and frozen; thaw only what you need, counting on six to eight pieces total per person.

HA GOW (make ahead and re-steam)
STEAMED SPARERIBS (make ahead and re-steam)
STEAMED BAO (make ahead and re-steam)
SAVORY FILLED PANCAKES (make ahead, pan-fry at the last minute)
TARTS, your choice (make ahead)

RICE IN LOTUS LEAF PACKETS (make ahead and re-steam)
CRAB DUMPLINGS (make ahead and re-steam)
CHAR SIU PASTRIES (freeze ahead and bake at the last minute)
MANGO PUDDING (make ahead and refrigerate)

SCALLOP DUMPLINGS (make ahead and re-steam)
POTSTICKERS, your choice (make ahead and freeze, pan-fry at the last minute)
BAKED CHAR SIU BAO (make ahead and reheat in the oven)
GREENS (blanch ahead, toss with dressing just before serving)
TARTS, your choice (make ahead)

SALT-FRIED WHOLE PRAWNS (prepare ahead, deep-fry at the last minute)
BAMBOO SHOOT DUMPLINGS (make ahead and re-steam)
PORK AND CHINESE CHIVE DUMPLINGS (make ahead and re-steam)
PEA SHOOTS WITH GARLIC (blanch, stir-fry at the last minute)
BAKED SWEET BAO, your choice (make ahead and reheat in the oven)

RICE FLOUR ROLLS WITH BEEF (some early preparation, last-minute cooking)
SAVORY TURNOVERS (freeze ahead and bake)

GREENS (blanch ahead, toss with dressing just before serving)
STUFFED BELL PEPPERS (prepare ahead, pan-fry at the last minute)
ALMOND PUDDING (make ahead and refrigerate)

DEEP-FRIED CRAB CLAWS (deep-fry up to 30 minutes ahead)
THREE-MUSHROOM DUMPLINGS (make ahead and re-steam)
RICE FLOUR ROLLS WITH BEAN SPROUTS (make up to 2 hours ahead)
BOILED BEEF DUMPLINGS (freeze ahead, boil at the last minute)
COCONUT BALLS (make several hours ahead)

EQUIPMENT AND SUPPLIES

Many common kitchen utensils and equipment may be used or adapted for making dim sum. A few pieces of equipment and supplies bear noting.

BAKING PANS, NONSTICK. 8 or 9 inches square. Essential for steamed, rolled rice flour sheets, so that the batter cooks with a smooth surface that does not adhere to the pan when being rolled up.

CANDY AND DEEP-FRYING THERMOMETER The thermometer clips to the side of a vessel and registers temperatures up to about 400°F. It is highly recommended to keep track of oil temperatures, which must be kept within a constant range for best results.

CHEESECLOTH Dampen several layers to line steamers when steaming breads. Cheesecloth absorbs moisture and keeps the breads from becoming waterlogged.

ENAMEL SAUCEPAN Use an enamel pan when a recipe contains vinegar or acidic ingredients, because acids may react with aluminum or other metals and give the food an off flavor.

FRYING PAN, ELECTRIC This is not essential equipment, but if you have a square electric frying pan with a tight-fitting lid, it is very useful for making rice flour rolls, which are prepared in baking pans floated over boiling water.

HEAT-PROOF DISHES These include round glass or stainless steel cake pans or pie plates, or ceramic or porcelain plates, about 8 to 9 inches in diameter.

PARCHMENT, BAKING Widely available in supermarkets. Squares of this are used under steamed items to keep them from sticking to the pan. Silicone-coated parchment may be used, but do not substitute waxed paper.

PASTRY BRUSH A soft pastry brush is invaluable for brushing egg-yolk glaze onto delicate pastries.

PLATE LIFTER (see page 18). Highly recommended if you use a steamer often.

ROLLING PINS A standard rolling pin works well for rolling out dumpling or pastry dough. In Asian kitchenware stores, you may also see miniature rolling pins, about 8 inches long and about 1 inch in diameter; they handle small rounds of dough well. You may also use a clean, straight-sided bottle, such as a wine bottle, or a thick, finely sanded dowel that has been lightly oiled with an edible oil.

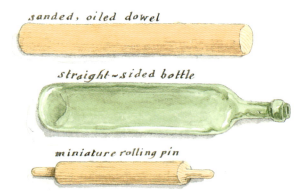

sanded, oiled dowel

straight-sided bottle

miniature rolling pin

SKILLET, NONSTICK Many recipes specify nonstick skillets for their ability to keep batter or dough from adhering and to use less oil. It needn't be heavy or expensive, but the surface should be unscratched.

STANDS (see page 18). Essential if you are devising a steamer from a pot.

STEAMERS (see page 17), metal or bamboo. Not necessarily expensive, but worth the cost if you do much steaming. The bottom part of a tiered metal steamer doubles as a pot.

STRAINERS A wire mesh strainer, available at many Asian kitchenware stores or Asian markets, has a heat-proof bamboo handle and a shallow bowl made from twisted brass-colored wire. Choose one that isn't too large for your wok or pot, but is big enough to hold what you are cooking. Mesh sieves may be used, too, and they are handy for scooping up stray bits from the oil when deep-frying. Slotted spoons may be used for smaller items, or together with a large strainer to hold large pieces of food.

TIMER Some digital timers can keep track of more than one time. It's especially useful when you are cooking dumplings, so that you don't lose track while you are shaping and steaming dumplings at the same time.

WOK WITH LID AND STAND Used to stir-fry, deep-fry, and steam. A carbon steel wok must be seasoned before it is used the first time. Stainless steel and nonstick woks do not require seasoning. Your wok should have a snug, domed lid that rests just inside the rim of the wok. It must allow room to accommodate a steamed dish on top of a stand (see page 17). A round-bottomed wok needs a special stand to stabilize the wok over a burner, absolutely essential if you use the wok for deep-frying. Most stands are ring-shaped, wider at the bottom than the top; large holes in the sides allow heat to escape. Buy the stand and lid at the same time you buy your wok so that you get matching sizes. Flat-bottomed woks do not require a stand.

RESOURCES

I have tried to keep the need for hard-to-find ingredients to a minimum, but some basic dim sum pantry items simply cannot be found outside Asian markets. For those items, I hope this limited list helps.

Besides the few resources listed here, many communities with an Asian population, whether Chinese or other, will have at least a small Asian market with items that may not be available at a supermarket or health food store. You may also want to check online for current companies that provide mail-ordered products.

GROCERIES AND SOME EQUIPMENT

Central Market
4001 N. Lamar
Austin, TX 78756
4821 Broadway
San Antonio, TX 78209
(800) 299-7046

EthnicGrocer.com
(Online only)

Ming.com
(Online only)

99 Ranch Market
(888) 910-8899 for customer service
Various northern California locations and
18230 East Valley Highway
Kent, WA 98032
(425) 251-9099

Quang Suong Food Company*
783 Clay Street
San Francisco, CA 94108
(415) 781-1520

Shun Fat Supermarket, Inc.
421 North Atlantic Boulevard
Monterey Park, CA 91754
(626) 308-3998, fax (626) 308-9072

S F Supermarket, Inc.
6930 65th Street, #123
Sacramento, CA 95823
(916) 392-3888, fax (916) 392-2888

T & T Supermarket, Inc.
179 Keefer Place
Vancouver, B.C., Canada V6B 6C1
(604) 899-6077

WIRE MESH STRAINER

KITCHEN EQUIPMENT

The Wok Shop*
718 Grant Avenue
San Francisco, CA 94108
(888) 780-7171
www.wokshop.com, available for online ordering

*You may place orders for groceries from Quang Suong Food Company; you must then call the Wok Shop (toll-free) to charge the order to a credit card. The Wok Shop will take care of shipping and handling for a nominal fee.

BIBLIOGRAPHY

I would like to acknowledge the following for invaluable bits of advice and insight. Some recipes are adapted from as many as eight or ten sources, for both ingredients and techniques, and I tasted more than 200 dishes to supplement what I read.

AU YANG, CECILIA J. *Chopsticks Recipes Dim Sum.* Hong Kong: Chopsticks Recipes Ltd., 1980.

————. *Chopsticks Recipes More Dim Sum.* Hong Kong: Chopsticks Recipes Ltd., 1994.

BLADHOLM, LINDA. *The Asian Grocery Store Demystified.* Los Angeles: Renaissance Books, 1999.

BLONDER, ELLEN, AND ANNABEL LOW. *Every Grain of Rice.* New York: Clarkson Potter/Publishers, 1998.

CHOW, KIT, AND IONE KRAMER. *All the Tea in China.* San Francisco: China Books and Periodicals, Inc., 1990.

CORRIHER, SHIRLEY O. *Cookwise.* New York: William Morrow and Co., Inc., 1997.

DAHLEN, MARTHA. *A Cook's Guide to Chinese Vegetables.* Hong Kong: The Guidebook Company Ltd., 1992.

HAHN, EMILY. *The Cooking of China.* New York: Time-Life Books, 1968.

HOM, KEN. *Asian Vegetarian Feast.* New York: Quill/William Morrow and Co., Inc., 1988.

HSIUNG, DEH-TA. *The Chinese Kitchen.* New York: St. Martin's Press, 1999.

HUANG SU-HUEI. *Chinese Cooking for Beginners.* Taipei: Wei-Chuan Publishing, 2000.

————. *Chinese Seafood.* Taipei: Wei-Chuan Publishing, 1995.

————. *Chinese Snacks.* Taipei: Wei-Chuan Publishing, 1999.

HUA, JIN. *Small Steamed Buns.* (Translation from Chinese) Taipei: Dee Ten Publishing Co., Ltd., 2000.

————. *Water Dumplings.* (Translation from Chinese) Taipei: Dee Ten Publishing Co., Ltd., 1988.

LEE, CHANG PING-CHIN. *Guangdong Dim Sum.* (Translation from Chinese) Guangzhou: Guangdong Hi-Tech Publisher, 1996.

————. *Guangdong Desserts and Snacks.* (Translation from Chinese) Guangzhou: Guangdong Hi-Tech Publisher, 1996.

LEE, HUA LIN. *Chinese Dim Sum.* Taipei: Chin Chin Publishing Co., Ltd., 1993.

————. *Vegetarian Cooking.* Taipei: Chin Chin Publishing Co., Ltd., 1996.

LILEY, VICKI. *Dim Sum.* Hong Kong: Periplus Editions, Ltd., 1999.

MOCK, LONNIE. *Dim Sum Cookbook.* Walnut Creek, California: Alpha Gamma Arts, 1977.

SO, YAN KIT. *Yan Kit's Classic Chinese Cookbook.* New York: Dorling Kindersley, Inc., 1995.

WU, WEN. *Peking Homestyle Noodle Dishes.* (Translation from Chinese) Taipei: Taiwan Co., Ltd., 2000.

YEE, RHODA. *Dim Sum.* San Francisco: Taylor & Ng, 1977.

INDEX